Jennifer Bauer &
Margarete Seidenspinner

Betriebswirtschaft: Übersetzungsübungen

Fachsprache Englisch

studium
kompakt

mergers

Fusionen

Cornelsen
& OXFORD

studium kompakt Fachsprache Englisch

Betriebswirtschaft: Übersetzungsübungen

Die Hochschulreihe studium kompakt Fachsprache Englisch wurde
von den Verfasserinnen und Verfassern in Zusammenarbeit mit der
Verlagsredaktion entwickelt.

Verfasserinnen:	Jennifer Bauer
	Prof. Dr. Margarete Seidenspinner
Verlagsredaktion:	Dr. Blanca-Maria Rudhart
Layout:	Gisela Hoffmann
Technische Umsetzung:	Sabine Theuring
Umschlagsgestaltung:	Grafik Design Vera Bauer, Berlin
Fotos:	Bavaria (Innenumschlag), S. 54; Corel Library

Die Deutsche Bibliothek – CIP-Einheitsaufnahme:
Bauer, Jennifer/Seidenspinner, Margarete:
studium kompakt Fachsprache Englisch:
Betriebswirtschaft: Übersetzungsübungen/Jennifer Bauer,
Margarete Seidenspinner. –
   1. Aufl. – Berlin: Cornelsen & Oxford University Press GmbH & Co., 2001
   ISBN 3-8109-3121-7

 http://www.cornelsen-teachweb.de

1. Auflage ✓ €

5	4	3	2	1	Die letzten Ziffern bezeichnen Zahl
05	04	03	02	01	und Jahr des Druckes.

Gesamtherstellung: Druckerei zu Altenburg

Bestellnummer 31217

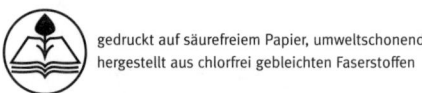 gedruckt auf säurefreiem Papier, umweltschonend
hergestellt aus chlorfrei gebleichten Faserstoffen

Contents

> Some hold translations not unlike to be
> the wrong side of a Turkish tapestry.

James Howell, the author of these lines, lived in post-Elizabethan England. But although the English language has changed considerably since then, the fundamental difficulties which are encountered when attempting to transfer linguistic concepts from one culture to another have remained; indeed, they have multiplied in the post-industrial age owing to the vast amount of new terminologies that are constantly being created.

This volume is intended for higher intermediate and advanced-level students aiming to improve their German-English translation skills and their competence in the area of business communication. It is suitable for independent learners at university/college level, as well as for professional people, and also for use by teachers of business English classes at institutions of higher or vocational education.

Translating has always required a high level of bilingual proficiency, as this is instrumental in unravelling the snags involved in the source as well as the target language. Natural languages are intricate artefacts, and one could argue that translating them is a task deserving professional expertise and attention (which indeed it is), as the translator has to convey the words – a challenge in itself – as well as their underlying cultural background and implied meanings. On the other hand, it is equally incontrovertible that, in practice, translating occurs every day and at all levels of secondary language acquisition.

In designing this workbook, the authors had a number of didactic aims in mind. These were, firstly, to raise students' level of awareness with regard to Anglo-American business terminology and usage patterns; secondly, to encourage the use of English terms, phrases and constructions which tend to be avoided by German speakers but which are essential to fluent and idiomatic translation; and, thirdly, to help learners to reduce the number of errors in their business writing, in particular those errors which result from linguistic interference.

Mistakes and misunderstandings in business language can be attributed to a variety of causes. These could be, for example, pseudo-English terms used in German (e.g. "mailings") or 'false friends' (e.g.

"Please sign on the backside."). Other problems may be less obvious – learners are often unaware of the complexity concealed in their own language, or they do not perceive different patterns in the target language. In addition, if they lack the specific terminology typically employed in Anglo-American business organisations, they may opt for simplistic semantic solutions which might serve the purpose of conveying basic ideas or messages but, in a professional context, will fail to produce even the wrong side of Howell's tapestry.

College and university students in particular often find translation classes difficult and frustrating because translation into English is presented as a daunting task that can only be mastered by native speakers. Translation exercises can help students to overcome this hurdle if they provide the kind of practice which raises their general level of linguistic awareness and deepens their interest in their own as well as the foreign language. For this reason, each text is accompanied by extensive annotations as well as transfer exercises which highlight specific areas of difficulty.

This book has been shaped by a pragmatic approach, which is to look at business terminology in the context in which it is generated and applied. German texts which reflect recent terminological tendencies in a range of subject areas have therefore been chosen. Where appropriate, the annotations include explanations of neologisms and buzzwords, which are frequently connected to management fashions and can often only be understood from within the cultural context in which they arise. Some of the differences between German and Anglo-American organisational structures and business practices are also indicated. In this area, students will find that distinctions which are of paramount importance in some cultures are of little relevance in others and that terms which have a narrow and precise definition in one business environment are used very loosely in another. Such information is indispensable to the translator who wishes to make an informed decision about how best to render a German business concept into English.

On a syntactic level, there are many challenges to be faced, too. Thus, for example, the pattern of the original German often has to be considerably changed in order to produce clear and comprehensible sentences in English. The 'Notes on the translation' therefore also include suggestions on techniques which facilitate this task. These notes are intended for students of business disciplines rather than linguists. Grammatical terms are used sparingly, and a glossary provides brief definitions of these terms. Where necessary, semantic differences between British and American usage are focussed on; however, spelling variants are not included, as these are well covered by the standard works of reference.

The authors of this book have a linguistic as well as a business background. Jennifer Bauer, who was born and educated in England, worked as a language consultant for a number of German companies before being appointed *Lektorin* for Business English at Mannheim University. Margarete Seidenspinner has completed English and Business Studies at British, German and South African universities. She also lectures in these subjects at the Fachhochschule Worms and at Mannheim University.

Acknowledgements

We are greatly indebted to our late colleague, Paul Jackson of Mannheim University, who first proposed the idea for this volume. We would further like to record our gratitude to Paul A. Cooper for performing the painstaking task of proof-reading and for providing valuable criticism and comments on the linguistic issues dealt with in the book.

Our thanks are also due to those students at Mannheim University and the Fachhochschule Worms who have participated in our business English classes and whose questions and feedback substantially contributed to the development of this material.

I   Telephone Banking

I.1 Text: Mit dem
Hörer in der Hand
die Finanzen fest
im Griff

I Telephone Banking

Mit TelefonBanking regeln Sie schnell und bequem alle Geldgeschäfte. Rund um die Uhr, sieben Tage die Woche.

TelefonBanking ist ein kostenloser 24-Stunden-Service für Ihr Privatgirokonto. Montags bis freitags von 7 bis 22 Uhr und samstags von 9 bis 16 Uhr nehmen unsere Mitarbeiter Ihre Aufträge persönlich entgegen. Außerhalb dieser Zeiten können Sie die gekennzeichneten Funktionen nutzen: Überweisungen*, letzte Umsätze*, Kontostand*, aktuelles Angebot*, Wertpapieraufträge, Daueraufträge, Adressänderungen, Versand von Kontoauszügen, Scheckanforderungen, Bestellung von EC- oder Kreditkarten und andere Aufträge. Der Zugang ist durch Ihre persönliche Geheimzahl gesichert.

(*Ein guter Draht zum Geld*/Landesbank Baden-Württemberg)

With your phone[1] in your hand you have your finances firmly under control[2]

With TelephoneBanking you can **carry out[3]** all your **banking transactions[4]** quickly and **smoothly[5]**. Round the clock, **seven days a week[6]**. TelephoneBanking is a **free[7]** 24-hour service for your personal **current account[8]**. **Mondays to Fridays[9] from 7 am to 10 pm[10]**, and on Saturdays from 9 am to 4 pm, our **staff[11]** will **deal with[12]** your **instructions[13] in person[14]**. Outside these hours you can **make use of[15]** all of the following functions which are marked with an asterisk (*): **credit transfers[16]***, details of latest **account transactions[17]***, statement of account balance*, **details of our current special offers[18]***, **orders to buy or sell securities[19]**, **standing orders[20]**, notification of changes of address, requests for the **mailing[21]** of **account statements[22]**, requests for **cheques[23]**, orders for **bank cards[24]** or credit cards, other instructions. Access is **protected[25]** by your personal **PIN number[26]**.

I.2 Sample translation

2.1 Notes on the translation

[1]   *Hörer:* phone; telephone

> 'With the receiver *(Hörer)* in your hand' is a more direct translation. However, in this heading, 'receiver' might not be immediately clear. It has a number of other meanings, e.g. *Konkursverwalter, Hehler, Empfänger* and 'telephone receiver' is unnecessarily long. '(Tele)phone' is more idiomatic, too.

← Please note

[2]   *die Finanzen fest im Griff:* you have your finances firmly under control; you have a firm grip on your finances

> Note in these phrases the use of the personal pronouns 'you/your' as opposed to the definite articles in German.

← Please note

[3]   *regeln:* carry out; effect; make; complete

> *Regeln* is used here in the sense of *abwickeln, erledigen.*
> Other translations of *regeln* are:
> - 'handle', 'take care of', 'deal with': *in die Hand nehmen, erledigen*
> - 'regulate', 'direct', 'control': *regeln, steuern*
> - 'regulate' also means 'monitor', 'oversee': *kontrollieren, überwachen.*
> - 'govern': *bestimmen, regieren, herrschen über*
> - 'guide', 'determine': *steuern*

●●●●●●●●

> • 'settle', 'put in order': *(endgültig) regeln, in Ordnung bringen*
> Common collocations are 'to settle one's financial affairs', 'to put one's financial affairs in order'.

[4] *Geldgeschäfte:* banking transactions
Geldgeschäfte in a non-banking sense may also be rendered as 'financial transactions'; 'money dealings'; 'money transactions'.

Please note →

> 'Business(es)' would be incorrect. For the usage of 'business' as a countable and non-countable noun see III.2.1, note [14], p. 44; and IV.2. 1, note [16], p. 58.

[5] *bequem:* smoothly; without fuss; at your own convenience

Please note →

> *Bequem and komfortabel* can be difficult to translate into English. Common equivalents are 'convenient', 'comfortable' or 'easy' (depending on the meaning of *bequem*), but often a more idiomatic solution is required, as suggested here.

For additional practice see I.3.3, Exercise 1: Adverbs and adjectives, p. 20.

[6] *sieben Tage die Woche:* seven days a week
not 'the week'. For additional practice on Adverbials of time see I.3.3, Exercise 2, p. 20.

[7] *kostenlos:* free; no-charge; charge-free

Please note →

> 'Free of charge' is always postpositive, i.e. placed after the noun it refers to, and would therefore not fit very easily into this sentence.

Examples of how this phrase could be used
TelephoneBanking is a 24-hour service which is free of charge.
We provide a 24-hour service free of charge.

[8] *Girokonto:* current account (GB); checking account (US)
[9] *montags bis freitags:* Mondays to Fridays
See I.3.3 for additional practice on Adverbials of time.
[10] *von 7 bis 22 Uhr:* from 7 am to/till 10 pm; from 07.00 to 22.00, from 7 in the morning till 10 in the evening

Please note →

> The combination '10 o'clock pm' is **incorrect**. Say instead: '10 pm' or '10 o'clock in the evening'.

Please note →

> Note that the twenty-four hour clock is uncommon, except in the military forces and in aviation. Please use the 24-hour clock as follows:

> Write '22.00' and pronounce this as 'twenty-two hundred' or 'twenty-two hundred hours'. **Never** say '22 o'clock'.

[11] *Mitarbeiter:* staff; service personnel; employees; personnel; members of staff

> - 'Staff' is used when referring to bank employees or service personnel but it is by no means an exclusive term for this group of people. It may translate broader terms such as *Personal, Belegschaft, Arbeitskräfte.*
> - 'Workers' is not normally associated with employees who provide a customer service (cf. also 'sales staff', 'counter staff') and would certainly be inappropriate here. However, this term does not always refer specifically to blue-collar workers or manual workers. We speak, for instance, of 'knowledge workers', when referring to people who work in information technology.

> Note that 'staff', like 'personnel', is a collective noun that has no plural form and cannot be preceded by an indefinite article. It is followed by a plural verb form.
> Example
> The staff were given a pay increase on January 1st.

← Please note

> Other translations for *Mitarbeiter* are 'colleague', 'co-worker', 'fellow worker'. All these terms would designate somebody you work together with.
> Example
> On his industrial placement, he soon found out that his English colleagues expected him to join them for a drink in the pub after work.
> More specific translations of *Mitarbeiter* are 'contributor' (especially on a newspaper or magazine) and 'collaborator' (especially on an academic project or a book). A 'collaborator', like *Kollaborateur,* can also be a person who co-operates with the enemy.

[12] *entgegennehmen:* deal with
'Receive' or 'accept' would be inappropriate here: These verbs do not convey, as *entgegennehmen* does, that any action will follow.

[13] *Aufträge:* instructions

In this context, 'instructions' is the best translation of *Aufträge* in the sense of *Anweisungen*. It is preferable to 'orders', as the latter has a variety of meanings (see X.2.1, note [11], p. 137); see also notes [19] and [20] below.

> Other possible translations of *Auftrag*, in the sense used here:
> - 'Task', 'job' (also used for *Auftrag* in data processing), 'assignment', 'duty' would all normally refer to a defined piece of work or job given to a specific person or group of people.
>
> Example
>
> Her assignment was to establish contacts with distributors in South East Asia.
> - 'Mission' is an assignment / an order carried out in a military or diplomatic context. The well-known phrase 'Mission accomplished!': *Auftrag ausgeführt!* is a humorous way of informing someone that a task has been completed. In business organisations, 'mission' is often synonymous with 'vision' (see VI.2.1, note [15], p. 82).
> - 'Commission' indicates a specified job, duty or power officially given to a person or a group of people.
>
> Example
>
> A German firm of architects received the commission to design the bank's new headquarters.
>
> Other useful phrases
>
> *im Auftrag von:* on the instructions of; at the request of; by order of; on behalf of
>
> *im Auftrag von jemandem handeln:* to act on behalf of somebody; to act on somebody's behalf
>
> *einen Auftrag erteilen, jemandem etwas auftragen:* to give instructions for something to be done; to instruct/tell somebody to do something

[14] *nehmen ... persönlich entgegen:* deal with ... in person, deal personally with

[15] *nutzen:* make use of; use

> 'Make use of' often collocates with abstract concepts, e.g. 'make use of our services' and also carries the meaning of 'take advantage of'

14

> 'Use' (nutzen, anwenden, einsetzen) simply means to employ something for a purpose and is therefore more likely to collocate with concrete things.
> Examples
> She uses a bike to get to work.
> We'll use the standard DTP software for this.

● ● ● ● ● ● ● ●
← Please note

16 *Überweisung:* credit transfer; credit transmission; credit remittance; giro transfer (GB); bank giro (GB)

> All these terms imply 'cashless money transfers': *bargeldlose Überweisungen.* By contrast, 'money transfers', i.e. *Geldüberweisungen,* are made by post. Both can be called a 'remittance' although this term actually denotes the 'money that is sent'.
> In GB, the giro system is the system which allows funds to be transferred from one bank account to another.

17 *letzte Umsätze:* (details of) latest account transactions; latest account movements; details of account credits and debits.
Umsätze means *Kontobewegungen* here, and 'details of' simply signifies 'information on'.
Umsatz also indicates the 'amount of goods or services sold by a company', i.e the 'turnover' (GB) or the total 'sales' as well as the actual 'sales revenues' *(Umsatzerlöse).*
Other useful terms
umsatzloses Konto: inactive account; dormant account
Gutschrift: credit (to an account)
Lastschrift: debit (to an account)

18 *aktuelles Angebot:* (details of our) current special offer(s), details of financial services currently offered, services currently on offer

← Please note

> *Angebot* here implies some particular financial service(s) or financial product(s) currently being promoted by the bank, in other words, it refers to the 'thing(s) offered': the noun 'offer', used alone would not make this clear here.
> Used by itself, 'offer' indicates:
> • the 'sum offered'
>   Their first offer was too low.
> • a statement offering to do something
> Further useful expressions
> We are open to offers: *Wir sind bereit, über den Preis zu verhandeln.*

●●●●●●●●

Is this a cash offer? *Bieten Sie Barzahlung an?*
We will make them an offer they cannot refuse: *Wir machen ihnen ein Angebot, das sie nicht ablehnen können.*
This notorious phrase was coined in the film 'The Godfather' and has subsequently been used when an 'offer' implies coercive tactics.

[19] *Wertpapieraufträge:* orders to buy or sell securities; commissions to buy or sell securities; instructions for purchases or sales of securities

Please note →

Strictly speaking, 'securities' is the correct translation of *Wertpapiere*. It is a generic name applied to various kinds of investment items like 'stocks' *(Wertpapiere mit festem Zinssatz, Effekten)*, 'shares' (US: 'stocks', i.e. *Aktien*), 'bonds' *(Anleihen, Obligationen, Schuldverschreibungen)* or 'debentures' *(gesicherte Anleihen, Obligationen, Schuldverschreibungen)*.
In everyday language, the term 'stocks and shares' is synonymous with 'securities' although this has to be considered as "loose usage".

[20] *Dauerauftrag:* standing order; banker's order
[21] *Versand* (i.e. *das Versenden von Post*): mailing; forwarding; posting (GB); sending
For the translation of *Lieferung* see XI.2.1, note [21], p. 151; for 'mail order' see II.2.1, note [19], p. 30.
[22] *Kontoauszug:* account statement; statement of account; bank statement
[23] *Scheck:* cheque (GB); check (US)
[24] *ec-Karten:* bank cards

'Bank card' is a fairly general term, not a translation of *ec-Karten* as such. In the US, a 'bank card' is used to obtain money from an automated teller machine (also known as 'ATM', 'cash machine', 'cash point', 'cash dispenser') or as a 'check guarantee card', in GB it is usually a 'cheque guarantee card' but could also be any kind of 'plastic bank card'. Some of the cards issued by banks are:
- 'eurocard' (GB): a legitimation card for eurocheques; also used to obtain money from a cash dispenser
- 'cheque (guarantee) card' (GB): *Scheckkarte*
- 'cash card' *(Geldautomatenkarte)*: used to obtain money from a cash dispenser

16

> - 'debit card': debits the holder's account immediately through a computer system. It may be used to purchase goods or services or to obtain money from a cashpoint.

[25] *gesichert:* protected; safeguarded

> - 'Protect' is mainly used in its transitive form
>   Example
>   You can protect your savings by putting them into a reputable investment fund.
>   'Protected access' is a common collocation with regard to security and computer security.
> - 'Safeguard' may also be used intransitively.
>   Example
>   We have to safeguard against industrial espionage.
> - 'Secure' usually signifies 'make safe', 'remove the threat of danger'.
>   Example
>   With the acquisition of Rover Cars, the consortium hoped to secure the future of the British car industry.
>   In finance, 'secure' is 'give a (legal) guarantee that something will be paid back', e.g. 'a secured loan': *ein gesichertes Darlehen.*
> - 'Save', in data processing, means 'store information': *Daten sichern, speichern.*
>   Example
>   The document was not saved and has thus been lost.
> - 'Cover' means 'protect from loss', 'insure': *sichern, (sich) absichern, decken, abdecken, versichern.*
>   Example
>   Are you covered against theft?
>   For the multiple semantic aspects of *Sicherheit* see XI.2.1 note [8], p. 150.

[26] *persönliche Geheimzahl:* (personal) pincode, (personal) PIN (number), secret PIN (number)
Note that 'PIN' stands for 'Personal Identification Number'.

3.1 Terminology: banking

1 Complete the sentences below by using the appropriate terms from the sample translation and the notes.

1 If a customer has regular fixed payments to make, like monthly rentals or insurance premiums, a ___ ___ *(Dauerauftrag)* is particularly useful.

2 A ___ *(Kontoauszug)* is a printed record showing all the transactions affecting a customer's account.

3 With telephone or online banking, most routine banking transactions can be ___ ___ *(erledigt)* from the comfort of your own home.

4 Most people have their salary paid into a ___ ___ *(Girokonto)*, as this is easily accessible and convenient for everyday use.

5 I just wanted to see how much money was in my account, so I checked my ___ *(Kontostand)* at the machine inside the bank.

6 Hedges *(Kurssicherungen)* are measures to ___ *(sich absichern)* against fluctuations in prices or exchange rates.

7 Substantial investment will be needed in order to ___ *(sichern)* the company's future.

8 She spends much of her day on the telephone, as she is mainly involved with ___ *(Aktiengeschäfte)*.

2 Using a dictionary, find the correct English terms for the following.

(Bank)konto	(bank) account, banking account (US)
1 Sparkonto	___
2 Gemeinschaftskonto	___
3 Nummernkonto	___
4 Kontonummer	___
5 Kontoinhaber	___
6 Kreditkarte	___
7 Kreditinstitut	___
8 Kreditnehmer	___
9 Kreditrahmen	___
10 Überziehungskredit	___
11 Blankoscheck	___
12 Barscheck	___
13 Verrechnungsscheck	___
14 einen Scheck ausstellen	___
15 einen Scheck einlösen	___
16 Überweisungsauftrag	___

17 Überweisungsempfänger ___
18 Überweisungsformular ___
19 Überweisungsgebühr ___
20 Überweisungsverkehr ___
21 Wertpapiere ___
22 Wertpapieranlage ___
23 Wertpapierdepot ___
24 Wertpapierverwaltung ___
25 Wertpapierberatung ___

3.2 Tricky translations

1 Words easily confused

Using both monolingual and bilingual dictionaries, find an English definition and a German translation of the <u>underlined</u> words.

1 a secured loan
2 a secure foothold in the market
3 a safe investment
4 to save money
5 to save the company from bankruptcy
6 to secure all the doors and windows
7 to lose your savings
8 this is good news for savers with building societies
9 the current balance on your account
10 the actual amount of money left
11 a range of special offers
12 the supply of consumer goods is very limited in this country
13 your request for a new chequebook
14 your instructions regarding the closing of your account

2 At the counter

Please translate:

1 Wir regeln gerne Ihre Geldgeschäfte.
2 Unsere Filiale wird Ihre Wertpapieraufträge entgegennehmen.
3 Wurden unsere Mitarbeiter über die On-line-Richtlinien informiert?
4 Speichern Sie bitte die neuen Adressen.
5 Mit Ihrer Bankkarte können Sie jederzeit unseren Geldautomaten nutzen.
6 Ist meine letzte Überweisung schon auf dem Bankauszug vermerkt?

7 Ihr Konto war im letzten Jahr vollkommen umsatzlos. Wollen Sie es nicht schließen?

8 Wie kann ich meine Ersparnisse besser schützen?

9 Bitte führen Sie unsere Anweisungen genau aus.

3.3 Additional practice
1 Adverbs and adjectives
Examples
She did the job quickly and efficiently. She is a quick and efficient worker.
She got an immediate pay rise. She got the pay rise immediately.
You can check the spelling very easily - just click on the icon at the top.
Online banking is a convenient way of managing your everyday finances.
Make sure you have the right forms, and check that you have filled them in correctly.

Please translate:

1 Während der Geschäftszeiten können Sie persönlich mit einem unserer Mitarbeiter sprechen.

2 Sie können gerne ein persönliches Gespräch mit unserer Filialleiterin vereinbaren.

3 Der Telefon-Computer versteht Sie am besten, wenn Sie deutlich und nicht zu langsam sprechen.

4 Sie sollten Ihre Geheimzahl unverzüglich ändern.

5 Sie brauchen die richtige Kontonummer.

6 Sie haben das Formular nicht richtig ausgefüllt.

7 CyberCash bietet ein sicheres, schnelles und äußerst komfortables Zahlungssystem.

8 Die notwendige Software erhalten Sie kostenlos und bequem aus dem Internet.

2 Adverbials of time
Examples
Seven days a week. Closed on Sundays. 24 hours a day. From nine till five. Eight am till four pm (On) weekdays. (At) weekends. In the mornings. Open every day/daily. Every night/nightly. From dusk till dawn.

Please translate:

1 morgens um sieben bis nachmittags um drei
2 fünf Tage die Woche
3 24 Stunden geöffnet
4 mittwochs geschlossen
5 jeden Abend von 18.00 bis 23.00
6 an Wochenenden geöffnet
7 von Sonnenaufgang bis Sonnenuntergang
8 täglich von 10.00 bis 22.00
9 sonntags nie

II   The Postal Service

II The Postal Service

II.1 Text: Der Brief: Fit für die Kommunikation der Zukunft

Allen elektronischen Medien zum Trotz: Der Brief ist und bleibt das wichtigste schriftliche Kommunikationsmittel. Er ist – auf Ihrem Geschäftspapier geschrieben und von Hand unterzeichnet – authentisch, persönlich und individuell. Der Empfänger erhält ein Originaldokument, dem besonderer Beweiswert zukommt. Kurz: Ein Brief schafft und pflegt beste Verbindungen – vertraulich, zuverlässig und seriös. Modernes Produktmanagement und ein High-Tech-gesteuertes Logistik-System haben den Brief fit für die Zukunft gemacht. Beispiel: die zuverlässigen Laufzeiten, die immer besser werden. Auch das Produkt- und Leistungsspektrum wird kontinuierlich weiterentwickelt – entsprechend Ihren Anforderungen und Bedürfnissen.

Briefprodukte für besondere Anforderungen

Sie wollen die Vorteile modernen Direktmarketings mit der Deutschen Post nutzen? Sie wollen größere Mengen inhaltsgleicher Sendungen, Warenmuster, Bücher, Broschüren oder Kataloge versenden? Wir haben für Sie die richtige Lösung: preis-leistungsstarke Brief-Produkte für bestimmte Versandwünsche.

Infopost

Die günstige Versandlösung für inhaltsgleiche Sendungen (z.B. Mailings oder Kataloge), die nach Postleitzahlen in auf- oder absteigender Reihenfolge geordnet sind:
– mindestens 4.000 Stück
– oder mindestens 250 Stück für dieselbe Leitregion (Übereinstimmung der ersten beiden Stellen der Postleitzahl)
– oder mindestens 50 Stück für den Leitbereich der Einlieferungsstelle.

Infobrief

Bei mindestens 50 inhaltsgleichen Sendungen (z. B. Einladungen) können Sie mit dem Infobrief auch ohne Vorsortierung nach Postleitzahl Porto sparen.

Warensendung

Warenproben oder Muster landen mit der Warensendung zuverlässig und günstig bei Ihren Kunden – in den Formaten Warensendung -Standard, -Kompakt oder -Maxi.
(*Der Brief: Schnell und leistungsstark für Ihren Versand*/Deutsche Post AG)

The letter: fit for the communication of the future

Despite all the electronic media available today[1], the letter still is and will remain the most important **medium of written communication**[2]. Written on your **company's notepaper**[3] and signed by hand, **it is authentic, personal and individual**[4]. The **addressee**[5] **receives**[6] an **original document**[7] which has special value as legal evidence[8]. **In short**[9], a letter creates and maintains the best **contacts**[10]: It is confidential, **reliable**[11] and **professional**[12].

Modern product management and a **technically sophisticated logistics system**[13] have made the letter fit for the future. Take, for example, the **delivery times**[14], **which are** reliable and **constantly improving**[15]. And the whole **range**[16] of products and **services**[17] **is** also **being continually improved and updated**[18] – in accordance with your requirements and needs.

II. 2 Sample translation

Letter products for specific requirements

Do you wish to make use of the advantages of modern **direct marketing**[19] with the help of **the German Postal Service**[20]? Do you need to send large quantities of **same-content mail**[21], **trade samples**[22], books, brochures or **catalogues**[23]? We have the right solutions for you: **excellent value**[24] letter products for your specific mailing **needs**[25].

Info-mail

The **cost-effective**[26] **solution**[27] for same-content mail (e.g. **mailshots**[28] or catalogues) which is sorted **by postcode**[29], in ascending or descending order:

- **4,000 items**[30] and above
- or 250 items and above for the same postal area (defined by the first two digits of the postcode)
- or 50 items and above for the postal district in which the letters are **posted**[31].

Info-letter

If you have 50 or more letters with the same contents (e.g. invitations), you can use the info-letter to **save on**[32] **postage**[33] – without even having to pre-sort your letters by postcode.

Trade samples mail[34]

With this form of mail, patterns or samples are delivered reliably and at low cost to your customers – in any of the three sizes available: standard, compact or maxi.

2.1 Notes on the translation

[1] *allen elektronischen Medien zum Trotz:* despite all the electronic media available today; in spite of all the electronic media available today; all the electronic media notwithstanding

Zum Trotz is used here in the same way as the preposition *trotz*, so the dictionary translation 'in defiance of' would not be correct here. 'Defiance' implies 'disobedience', i.e. *Ungehorsam*.

Examples

In defiance of my orders, he destroyed the documents.

The staff acted in defiance of the boss.

'Notwithstanding' is somewhat more formal than 'despite' or 'in spite of' and appears directly after the noun it refers to.

Please note →

> Note that 'media' is a plural noun followed by a plural verb form. The singular form is 'medium' (see note [2]).
> Example
> The media are interested in our new product.

[2] *schriftliches Kommunikationsmittel:* medium of written communication; form / means of written communication

Further usage examples

an 'advertising medium' (e.g. T.V., radio, the press, Internet)

a 'means / form of transport' (e.g. car, train, plane)

Please note →

> Note that 'means' is a countable noun with both a singular and a plural form. For additional practice on singular and plural noun forms see II.3.3, Exercise 2, p. 37.

[3] *Geschäftspapier:* company('s) notepaper; company('s) stationery/ writing paper

'Company stationery' is the collective term for the paper, documents, cards, etc. with the company's letterhead *(Briefkopf)*, emblem or logo printed on them.

Please note →

> *Geschäftspapier* is not a lexical item that you are likely to find in a German-English dictionary. When translating such words (quite often encountered in company publicity, reports, etc.), one has to first consider the possible synonyms in German (e.g. *Briefpapier* in this case), and/or think of a definition in English (e.g. 'paper that companies use to write letters on').

> The plural form, *Geschäftspapiere*, is translated as 'commercial documents'. This denotes all the documents, papers, accounts, invoices and business records that exist in or are held by a company.

●●●●●●●●

4   *Er ist – auf Ihrem Geschäftspapier geschrieben – authentisch, persönlich und individuell:* Written on your company's notepaper, it is authentic, personal and individual.

> In English, additional information (e.g. an adverbial phrase) is not usually interjected into the middle of the clause but added at the beginning or end. It may, possibly, be interjected in brackets.

← Please note

5   *Empfänger:* addressee; recipient

← Please note

> - The 'addressee' is specifically the recipient of a letter or parcel. This term is preferred here because it avoids the awkward-sounding phrase 'The recipient receives ...'.
> - 'Receiver' and 'recipient' are possible translations, too. However, 'receiver' needs to be specified in order to make its meaning clear: the receiver of the parcel, the receiver of the consignment.
> - 'Recipient' is preferable to 'receiver' because of the polysemous nature of the latter which is explained in I.2.1, note [1], p. 11.

For 'consignee' see XI.2.1, note [21], p. 151.

6   *erhält:* receives
In this kind of text, the colloquial 'get' would be too informal.
For the difference in meaning between 'receive' and 'obtain' see VIII.3.2, Exercise 1, p. 114.

7   *ein Originaldokument:* an original document ; a source document
'Source documents' *(Originalbelege)* are documents such as invoices which evidence business transactions. In data processing, they are documents transcribed onto a computer *(Quelldokumente)*.

8   *dem besonderer Beweiswert zukommt:* which has special value as legal evidence; which has special value as evidence in law; which has particular evidentiary value / evidential value
'Proof' could be an alternative to 'evidence': Both terms mean 'a way of showing that something is true': *Beweis, Nachweis.*

Please note →

'Evidence' and 'proof' are uncountable, and if we want to translate the idea of *'ein Beweisstück'*, we would use 'piece/ item of evidence' (not 'proof').

Further examples of usage

proof of delivery: *Liefernachweis*

proof of damage: *Schadensnachweis*

proof of posting: *Einlieferungsschein*

evidence of shipment: *Verladebestätigung*

to give evidence in court: *vor Gericht aussagen*

You will need some documentary evidence/proof: *Sie werden einen schriftlichen Nachweis brauchen.*

Do you have any proof of your identity? *Können Sie sich ausweisen?*

[9] *kurz:* in short ...; to put it briefly ...

[10] *Verbindungen:* contacts

Please note →

- *Verbindung/Kontakt*
  die Verbindung/den Kontakt zu jemandem herstellen: to establish contact with someone
  (jede) Verbindung zu einer Person abbrechen: to break off (all) contact(s) with a person

- *Kontakte/Beziehungen*
  Sie musste ihre Beziehungen spielen lassen, um diesen Praktikumsplatz zu bekommen./Sie musste ihre Kontake nutzen, ... She had to use her connections/contacts to get that internship.
  In vielen Ländern braucht man Kontakte/Beziehungen auf höchster Ebene, um indirekte Handelsschranken zu umgehen. In many countries, one needs high-level contacts in order to bypass invisible trade barriers.
  For further practice see II.3.2 Tricky translations: words easily confused, Exercise 1, p. 35.

- *Beziehungen*
  'Relations', apart from denoting 'relatives', signifies 'personal, social or political connections and dealings between two or more members of a group'.
  Die beiden Länder haben stets gute Beziehungen unterhalten. The two countries have always enjoyed excellent relations.

> *Unsere Firma bemüht sich um langfristige Beziehungen zu ihren Kunden.* Our company seeks to establish long-term relations with its customers.

[11] *zuverlässig:* reliable
'Reliable' can be attributed to products and persons whereas 'dependable' and 'trustworthy' tend to be mainly applied to people.

[12] *seriös:* professional
Other translations of *seriös*, which would not, however, fit so well here, are 'reputable' (especially of a company) and 'respectable' (especially of a person of good standing in the community).

> A false friend: 'Serious(ly)' renders *'ernst', 'ernsthaft'*.

← Please note

[13] *ein High-Tech-gesteuertes Logistik-System:* a technically sophisticated logistics system; a high-tech logistics system
Gesteuert can often mean 'controlled', but the attribute *High-Tech-gesteuert* cannot be rendered directly into English, as 'high-tech' is an unchangeable modifier (see XII.3.3, Exercise 2, p.173). As a result, a rather long relative clause such as 'a logistics system which is controlled by sophisticated technology' would be required.

Further examples
privately controlled: *privat geführt*
state-controlled: *staatlich gelenkt/verwaltet*

> Note the 's'-ending in the singular noun logistics which can also form part of a compound, e.g. a logistics system, a logistics problem.

← Please note

[14] *Laufzeiten:* delivery times, lead times

> - 'Delivery time' is the time between posting and delivering *(zustellen)* a postal item. In industry, its counterpart, 'lead time' specifies the period between placing an order and receiving the product or the service.
> - 'Forwarding time' is the period in which merchandise is transported to its recipient. In the context of postal services, 'to forward' corresponds to *nachschicken, nachsenden*.
>   The nouns 'period', 'life', 'term' translate *Laufzeit* in connection with loans, contracts, insurance policies, etc.

← Please note

●●●●●●●● ¹⁵ *die immer besser werden:* which are ... constantly improving; which are ... continually improving; which are getting faster all the time

Please note →

Note the use of the continuous present tense in English to describe a current development which is emphasized by the adverb *immer* as an apposition to *besser, schlechter,* etc. in German, and by the adverbs 'continually' or 'constantly' in English.

¹⁶ *(Produkt- und Leistungs-)Spektrum:* range
'Product range/range of products' *(Sortiment, Produktpalette)* and 'range of services' *(Servicepalette, Serviceangebot)* are all common collocations.
'Spectrum' is unlikely to be used here.
It appears in expressions such as the following:
a broad spectrum of views/opinions
a wide spectrum of emotions/capabilities

¹⁷ *Leistungen:* services
One of the possible translations of *Leistungen* is services, especially when it signifies *Dienstleistungen, Dienste.* See note ²⁴ below for *Preis-Leistungsverhältnis*; VIII.2.1, note ⁷ p. 108 for *leistungsorientierte Entlohnung* and V.2.1, note ¹, p. 67 for *Spitzenleistungen.*

¹⁸ *wird kontinuierlich weiterentwickelt:* is being continually improved and updated; is being improved all the time; is being constantly improved
The combination of 'improved and updated' conveys best the idea implied by *weiterentwickelt.* For the usage of the continuous present tense see note ¹⁵.
'To develop something further' is most likely to translate *weiterentwickeln* in connection with the word 'idea'.
Example
Perhaps you could develop that idea further.

Please note →

'Continually' and 'constantly' both mean 'occurring regularly', 'happening frequently' over a certain period of time, whereas 'continuously' signifies 'without interruption', 'without a break'.

¹⁹ *Direktmarketing:* direct marketing
'Direct marketing' covers a variety of 'direct selling' *(Direktvertrieb, Direktabsatz)* measures, i.e. from the manufacturer directly to the customer bypassing all retail outlets or intermediaries.

For sales promotion, 'direct marketing' may employ, amongst other things, 'direct mail (advertising)' or 'direct mailing' *(Brief-werbung, Direktwerbung, Postversandwerbung)*. 'Direct mail' *(Direktversand)* is used by 'mail order companies' *(Versand-häuser)* which employ postal or telephone services, as well as the Internet.

Example

These CDs are exclusively sold by direct mail: *Diese CDs sind nur im Direktversand erhältlich.*

In e-commerce, the neologism 'e-tailing' (an analogy of 'retailing') is becoming increasingly popular.

20 *die Deutsche Post:* the German Postal Service; the German Post Office

← Please note

> A Post Office is a public authority responsible for postal servi-ces. In the US, the United States Postal Service (USPS) is the independent agency which deals with sending letters and parcels.
> Some of the services offered by post offices are:
> Post Office box: *Postfach*
> General Delivery (US), poste restante (GB): *postlagernd*
> business reply service: *Werbeantwort-Service*
> express mail: *Eilzustellung*
> money orders: *Postanweisungen, Zahlungsanweisungen*
> registered post/mail: *Einschreiben, Einschreibesendung*
> cash on delivery (COD, cod): *Nachnahme*

21 *inhaltsgleiche Sendungen:* same-content mail; bulk mail; the same type of mail

← Please note

> 'Bulk mail' *(Postwurfsendung)* is any mail (usually advertising material) sent out on a widespread basis, e.g. to all households in a certain area, or to all the addresses on a 'mailing list' *(Anschriftenliste)*.
> *Sendung* is a polysemous noun whose meanings include:
> * *Versenden/Verschicken (mit der Post)*, which can be render-ed as 'sending', 'mailing' or 'posting' (esp. in GB usage)
> * *Postsendung:* whose most appropriate equivalent is 'mail' as this means 'items sent by mail' (e.g. letters, parcels, packages)

Note that 'mail' is an uncountable noun.
An exception to this is 'e-mail'.
Send me an e-mail.
I had hundreds of e-mails to deal with.

Other useful expressions

eine Briefsendung: a letter
eine Paketsendung: a parcel, a consignment
eine eingeschriebene Sendung: a registered letter/parcel
noch nicht zugestellte Sendungen: parcels and letters awaiting delivery

22 *Warenmuster:* trade samples; samples of goods; commercial samples; merchandise samples; samples

23 *Kataloge:* catalogues (GB); catalogs (US)

24 *preis-leistungsstark:* excellent value; excellent value for money
The synonymous expression *ein gutes Preis-Leistungsverhältnis* corresponds to 'good value for money', 'good value', 'well worth the price'.

25 *Wünsche:* needs; requirements

The meanings of *Wünsche* include:
- need: *(Bedürfnis)*, as in the above text
- wish: something you desire *(Wunsch)* but cannot have at present
- request: something you ask for *(Bitte)*
- best wishes, e.g. on your birthday: *Glückwünsche*

Examples
Auf Wunsch schicken wir Ihnen unsere neueste Preisliste: We will send you our latest price list on request.
Please extend my best wishes to Paul: *Bitte übermitteln Sie Paul meine besten Wünsche.*

26 *günstig:* cost-effective; reasonably priced; low-cost; low-price

Example
We consider direct mailing a very cost-effective way of advertising.

'Cheap' would not be used in promotional corporate literature, as it has the same connotations as *billig*. Inexpensive products are sometimes humorously called 'cheap and cheerful'.

26 *Versandlösung:* solution
The direct rendering 'mailing solution' would be unorthodox. If a precise translation were necessary, it would be 'solution for your

mailing needs'. However, this would be both redundant and clumsy.

[27] *Mailings:* mailshots; mail shots; direct mail shots

> 'Mailing' is not used in English with an indefinite article or in the plural form. It is the gerund form of the verb denoting 'the activity of sending by mail', not the 'item sent'.

← Please note

See note [21] above for further translations of 'mail'/'mailing'.

[29] *nach Postleitzahlen geordnet:* sorted by postcode/zipcode (US); sorted according to (their) postcodes/zipcodes

[30] *4.000 Stück:* 4,000 items

> Note that thousands in English are marked by commas.

← Please note

> *Stück* has several distinct meanings. It may be:
> - a piece or separate item taken from/belonging to an uncountable quantity or a whole
>   Examples
>   a piece of furniture: *ein Möbelstück*
>   a piece of wood: *ein Stück Holz*
> - a non-countable quantity unit whose English equivalent is a countable noun
>   Examples
>   *3 Stück:* 3 items; 3 units
>   *20 Dollar das Stück:* 20 dollars each; 20 dollars per item
> - the first element of a composite noun
>   Examples
>   *Stücklohn:* piece rate
>   *Stückkosten:* unit costs

[31] *Einlieferungsstelle:* (the postal district) in which the letters are posted; ... where the letters are handed in for posting
See also note [8], p. 28 for *Einlieferungsschein.*

[32] *sparen:* save on; save; economise on
Examples
I saved £50 by flying economy class.
I saved a lot of money on postage.
You can save/economise on postage by taking advantage of the special rates.

[33] *Porto:* postage; postage charges; postal charges; mailing charges

34 *Warensendung:* trade samples mail; mailing of trade samples
Here, *Warensendung* appears to mean *das Versenden von Warenproben*. This is why 'trade samples mail' is the translation of choice.
For *Warenlieferung* see XI.2.1, note [21], p. 151.

3.1 Terminology: postal services

1 Complete the following sentences using words and phrases from the sample translation and the footnotes.

1 Post offices in most countries offer a ___ ___ *(breite Palette)* of services: ___ *(Zustellung)* of parcels and letters, banking services, business reply services, international money orders, ___ *(eingeschriebene Sendungen)* to name just a few.

2 Over the last ten years, the ___ ___ *(Dienstleistungsbranche)* has grown much more rapidly than the trade in goods.

3 Despite all the advantages of electronic communication, it seems likely that the 'traditional' letter will remain an important ___ *(Mittel)* of business communication in the foreseeable future.

4 Sending out a newsletter every month helps companies to ___ *(aufrechterhalten, pflegen)* ___ *(Verbindungen)* with their regular customers.

5 ___ *(vertrauliche)* information, such as pay advice, or anything else that concerns the individual employee only, should be ___ *(gesandt)* to the employee in a sealed ___ *(Briefumschlag)*.

6 Bulk mail and the ___ *(Versenden)* of ___ ___ *(Warenproben)* requires a certain quantity to be ___ *(kostengünstig)*.

7 Whenever you post a ___ *(Paket)*, make sure to keep the ___ *(Einlieferungsschein)* in case it gets lost.

8 ___ *(Laufzeiten)* for letters are becoming shorter and shorter.

2 Using a dictionary, find the correct equivalent for the following postal items.

	Luftpost	air mail
1	Postzustellung	____
2	Poststempel	____
3	frankierter Rückumschlag	____
4	Freiumschlag	____
5	portofrei	____
6	Auslandspostanweisung	____

  7 Werbeantwort   ____
  8 Antwortkarte   ____
  9 Rückantwortschein   ____
 10 Briefwechsel   ____
 11 Briefkopf   ____
 12 Brieftext   ____
 13 Kurzbrief   ____
 14 Postanschrift   ____
 15 Nachsendeanschrift   ____
 16 Empfänger   ____
 17 Absender, Adresse des Absenders   ____
 18 Kollo, Packstück, Paket   ____
 19 Paketpost   ____
 20 Paketzustellung   ____
 21 Eilpaket   ____

3.2 Tricky translations: words easily confused

1 Using monolingual and bilingual dictionaries, find an English definition and a German translation of the underlined words in the phrases given below.

 1 I'll contact you
 2 I'll connect you
 3 lose contact with a person
 4 have the right sort of connections
 5 a permanent workforce of twenty
 6 constant maintenance of the machines
 7 continually make mistakes
 8 employed continuously from January to July
 9 a very serious-looking judge
10 a professional-looking letter
11 a serious problem
12 a serious suggestion

2 Translate the following sentences. Include the words given in (brackets).

 1 Diese ständigen Unterbrechungen erschweren die Konzentration (make it difficult to).
 2 Ist 10 Downing Street Ihr ständiger Wohnsitz (address)?

3 Wir arbeiteten ohne Unterbrechung von 8 Uhr morgens bis 8 Uhr abends, um diese Aufgabe zu erledigen (to get this task finished).

4 Die Verkaufszahlen haben sich seit letztem Jahr kontinuierlich verbessert.

5 Sind diese Informationen zuverlässig?

6 Jack läßt dich bestimmt nicht im Stich (let you down); er ist äußerst zuverlässig.

7 Promex ist eine seriöse Firma und ein ernstzunehmender Mitbewerber um den Vertrag (contender for).

3.3 Additional practice

1 The continuous present
Examples
Our products are being improved all the time.
Electronic communication is becoming increasingly widespread.
We are constantly looking for ways to make the service more efficient.
Our delivery times are getting faster and faster.

(Deutsche Post AG)

36

Please translate:
1   Unsere Filialen werden ständig modernisiert.
2   Unser Geschäft wird zunehmend internationalisiert.
3   Diese Technologie wird ständig weiterentwickelt.
4   Der Markt für Dienstleistungen wächst immer schneller.
5   Seine beruflichen Leistungen werden immer besser.
6   Die Kosten gehen ständig in die Höhe.

2   Singular and plural forms
Examples
The news is up-to-date.
All the mail has to be sorted as soon as it arrives in the morning.
The evidence still has to be presented.
A bicycle is a means of transport which is often very efficient in towns.
The headquarters of our company are in Zürich.
The goods were delivered last week.

Please translate:
1   Die Beweise sind nicht eindeutig.
2   Ist die ganze Post hier für mich?
3   Die Ware wurde bisher noch nicht geliefert.
4   Wir haben fünfzig Stück bestellt.
5   Die elektronischen Medien ersetzen allmählich den traditionellen Brief.
6   E-mail ist eine elektronische Kommunikationsmöglichkeit, die viele nutzen.
7   Unsere Hauptgeschäftsstelle wurde nach London verlegt.
8   Sind diese Daten vertraulich?
9   Die Informationen waren nicht sehr hilfreich.

III Teleworking

III Teleworking

Grundsätzlich bedeutet Telearbeit, dass der Beschäftigte außerhalb des Betriebes arbeitet und dazu Informations- und Kommunikationstechniken benutzt. Mit der Firma verbunden ist der Telearbeiter per Computer, Telefon, Fax oder anderen Datenübertragungswegen. Je nachdem, wo der Arbeitsplatz liegt, lassen sich vier Formen von Telearbeit unterscheiden:

1 Tele-Heim-Arbeit bedeutet, dass der Schreibtisch ausschließlich in den eigenen vier Wänden des Beschäftigten steht.

2 Alternierende Telearbeit heißt, dass der Beschäftigte abwechselnd im heimischen Büro und im Betrieb arbeitet. Nach Ansicht von Unternehmensberater Hans-Ulrich List verhindert dies, dass der häusliche Arbeiter sozial isoliert wird. „Wenn wir Unternehmen und Behörden beraten, versuchen wir immer, von der reinen Telearbeit wegzukommen", sagt List. „Alternierende Telearbeit hat außerdem den Vorteil, dass Teams erhalten bleiben."
Eine Expertenrunde des Bundesministeriums für Bildung und Forschung stellte 1996 ebenfalls fest, dass eine Mehrheit von befragten Telearbeitern in Deutschland, anderen europäischen Ländern und den USA das alternierende System vorzieht: Statt nur zuhause zu arbeiten, wollten sie mindestens drei Tage im Betrieb beschäftigt sein. Hier muss nicht immer ein eigener zweiter Schreibtisch stehen. Möglich ist, laut Telearbeit-Spezialist List, auch „Desk Sharing": mehrere Telearbeiter, die an unterschiedlichen Tagen in der Firma sind, teilen sich einen Büroplatz.

3 Mobile Telearbeit gibt es schon länger als den Begriff: Sie wird von Außendienstbeschäftigten oder Servicetechnikern, die von Kunde zu Kunde fahren, geleistet. Auch Unternehmensberater, Wirtschaftsprüfer oder Softwareentwickler haben ihren Schreibtisch häufig für die Dauer eines Projektes oder eines Auftrages im Betrieb ihres Kunden stehen.

4 Arbeit in Tele- oder Servicezentren: hierfür bündelt der Arbeitgeber mehrere Telearbeitsplätze in Büros in der Nachbarschaft der Beschäftigten. Diese Art der ausgelagerten Arbeit ist in Deutschland – im Unterschied zu Großbritannien – bislang jedoch kaum zu finden.

(DM Online Karriere-*Spezial*
http://www.dm-online.de/karriere/telearbeit/telearbeit2.html)

Teleworking[1] – the trends

Telework basically means that[2] the employee works **outside the premises of an organisation**[3], **using**[4] **information technology and telecommunications**[5]. The teleworker is **linked with**[6] the company **by**[7] computer, telephone, fax or other means of **data transfer**[8]. Four forms of telework can be distinguished, according to where the **workplace**[9] **is located**[10].

III.2 Sample translation

1 **Home telework**[11] means that **the workplace is exclusively situated in the employee's own home**[12].
2 Alternating telework means that the employee works alternately **at home**[13] and **on the company's premises**[14]. In the view of **management consultant**[15] Hans-Ulrich List, **this prevents the home worker from becoming socially isolated**[16]. "When we are advising companies and public authorities, we always try to move away from the idea of home telework only", says List. "Alternating telework also has the advantage that teams can be maintained." In 1996, a group of experts from the **German Ministry**[17] of Education and Research also found that the majority of tele-workers interviewed in Germany, other European countries and the USA prefer the alternating system. **Rather than working only at home**[18], they want to work at least three days a week on the company's premises. **A second desk of one's own in the company is not always necessary**[19]. Telework specialist List says that "desk sharing" is also a possibility: this means that several teleworkers who are in the company on different days **share one office space**[20].
3 Mobile telework has existed longer than its name has. It is performed by **travelling salesmen**[21] or service engineers who travel from customer to customer. Management consultants, **company auditors**[22] or software developers also often work at a desk in their **client's**[23] offices for the duration of a project or a **commission**[24].
4 Work in telecentres or service centres. In this case the employer **groups together**[25] a number of **telework spaces**[26] in office buildings **in the employees' neighbourhood**[27]. **This type of work performed outside the company**[28] is, however, still very un-common in Germany[29] – **in contrast**[30] to Great Britain.

2.1 Notes on the translation

1 *Telearbeit:* teleworking, telework, telecommuting
2 *grundsätzlich bedeutet Telearbeit, dass:* telework basically means that; basically/in principle telework means that; telework means, basically/in principle, that

Please note →

> - 'Basic(ally)' and 'fundamental(ly)', which are both possible translations of *grundsätzlich*, may sometimes be synonyms, but 'fundamental(ly)' conveys an idea of 'profundity', 'seriousness', 'deep importance' *(grundlegend, fundamental)* and would not be the right translation here. 'Basically' conveys the idea of 'in its basic meaning'.
> - 'In principle': in general, in theory, as a rule.
> - 'On principle': as a matter of moral principle.

3 *außerhalb des Betriebes:* outside the premises of an organisation; outside the company's premises; at a distance from the company employing him or her; away from his or her company
4 *und dazu (Informationstechniken) benutzt:* using (information technology); and uses (information technology) for this work/for this purpose

Please note →

> Using a gerund form is often a good way of translating *'und ...'*-clauses when the subject is the same as in the main clause. The subject in both clauses here is 'the employee' *(der/die Beschäftigte).*
>
> A further example
> *Der Dollar erholte sich und machte zehn Punkte an den Devisenmärkten gut.* The dollar recovered, gaining ten points on the foreign exchange markets.

5 *Informations- und Kommunikationstechniken:* information technology and telecommunications; information technology and communications technology

Please note →

> **Do not** use a hyphenated form (information-), as this would be unclear.

6 *mit (der Firma) verbunden:* linked with/to; connected with/to
7 *(verbunden) per:* (linked) by; via
8 *Datenübertragung:* data transfer; data transmission
9 *Arbeitsplatz:* workplace; work place; place of work; workstation
The first three terms denote the (physical) location where a person is employed. A 'workstation' (also: 'work station') is an area within

a company or a home equipped with the tools needed (especially a computer, modem, telephone) for one person to do a specific job. For detailed comments on the translation of *Platz* see VII.3.2, p. 101.

10 *je nachdem, wo der Arbeitsplatz liegt:* according to where the workplace is situated; depending on where the workplace is located; depending on the location of the workplace
Other usages of 'according to' and 'depending on'
According to the annual report, sales rose to a new record figure. *Laut Geschäftsbericht erreichte der Umsatz einen neuen Rekordwert.*
The company is now depending on the government to rescue them. *Die Firma verlässt sich jetzt darauf, dass die Regierung sie rettet.*

11 *Tele-Heim-Arbeit:* home telework

> A 'home worker' ('homeworker') is any person who works from home, usually using some sort of equipment needed for the job, such as a sewing machine, a telephone or a computer. Traditionally, 'home work' *(Heimarbeit)* was often carried out by women, usually on a piecework basis.
> Similar terms are 'outworker' and 'outwork'. An 'outworker' is any person who works for an organisation outside the organisation's own premises. This term is mainly used in the 'garment trade' *(Bekleidungsindustrie)*, but, theoretically, could also be a translation of *Heimarbeiter* or *Telearbeiter*.

← Please note

> 'Home work' is written as two separate words, to distinguish it from 'homework' in the sense of 'schoolwork done at home' *(Hausaufgaben)*.
> 'Telework', like usually other compounds with tele-, is not usually hyphenated. (cf. compounds like 'teleconference', 'telemarketing', 'telesales'). It is thus unlikely that the German compound *Tele-Heim-Arbeit* would be directly translated as 'tele-home-work'. This looks odd in English, and the meaning is less clear than in the German version.

12 *der Schreibtisch steht ausschließlich in den eigenen vier Wänden des Beschäftigten:* the workplace is exclusively situated in the employee's own home; the workstation is exclusively located in the employee's own home; the employee works exclusively at home; the employee's desk is exclusively located in his or her own home

The German text probably uses *Schreibtisch* to avoid repeating *Arbeitsplatz* from the previous sentence, for reasons of style. However, this kind of repetition – for the sake of clarity – would not be considered to be stylistically deficient in English texts. In translating from German to English, it is sometimes even a good idea to 're-introduce' the repetition which has, presumably, been consciously avoided by the German author.

13 *im heimischen Büro:* at home, in his or her home office; in his or her home

> A 'home office', meaning an 'office in the home', is a relatively new term, which is becoming increasingly common. The 'SOHO' (small office, home office) sector is fast-growing. It comprises home workers and people who work in very small organisations consisting of just a couple of people.
> In Great Britain, the 'Home Office' (capital letters) is the ministry of the interior *(Innenministerium)*.

14 *im Betrieb:* on the company's premises; in the company, on the firm's premises, on the premises *(Firmengelände, Räumlichkeiten)* of the organisation/the business establishment employing him or her

Please note →

- *Betrieb* denotes, first and foremost, a 'place of production or product processing' (factory, plant, shopfloor) where the manual or 'blue-collar workers' used to be employed.
- In this sense, it differs from *Geschäft* (business) which is any organisation run for profit, a place of commerce.
  As the manufacturing sector lost some of its economic importance, *Betrieb* adopted a broader meaning. The following terms describe various types of businesses.
- 'Company' or 'corporation' (US), which is an all-inclusive term for all types of incorporated *(Kapitalgesellschaften)* as well as unincorporated undertakings *(Personengesellschaften)*.
  'Incorporated companies' possess a legal entity separate from that of their members and thereby represent a legal person in their own right. They include, for instance, 'private limited companies' (GB) or 'close corporations' (US) which correspond to *Gesellschaften mit beschränkter Haftung (GmbH)*, as well as 'public limited companies' (GB) or 'stock

corporations' (US) whose German counterparts are *Aktiengesellschaften*.

'Unincorporated companies' include 'trading partnerships' *(offene Handelsgesellschaften, OHG)*, whose individual partners each bear unlimited liability, as well as 'sole proprietors' or 'sole traders' *(Einzelkaufleute, Alleininhaber)* who run their own businesses. 'Sole proprietors' such as medical doctors, lawyers, auditors or consultants, who have their own professional practice, are referred to as 'sole practitioners'.

- 'Firm' strictly speaking, is a business partnership. In colloquial usage, this term is often a synonym for 'company'.
- 'Establishment' is a place run as a business (e.g. a restaurant) or for a special purpose (e.g. a 'research establishment': *Forschungseinrichtung*). The expression 'business establishment' seeks to distinguish a commercially-oriented set up from those that serve other purposes.
- '(Business) organisation' *(Gesellschaft)* is the collective term for all types of publicly and privately owned and administrated businesses *(Gesellschaften)*, although – in a more specific sense – it denotes a group of people who have come together for a specific purpose (e.g. the 'World Health Organization': *Weltgesundheitsorganisation*).
- 'Enterprise' is sometimes synonymous with 'business' and 'company' and the direct equivalent of *Unternehmen*. It is often employed as an official label, eg. for 'state enterprises' *(Staatsbetriebe, staatliche Unternehmen)* and for those commercial organisations that are privately owned or require some entrepreneurial initiative, e.g. 'small and medium-sized enterprises'.
  See V.2.1, note [28], p. 73.
  'Enterprise' strongly connotes 'business (ad)ventures' *(Unterfangen)* that involve an element of risk for their owners.
  See V.2.1, note [3], p. 67.
  'Undertaking' *(Unternehmung, Unterfangen)* is closely related to 'enterprise':
  The construction of the tunnel was a privately-financed undertaking.

[15] *Unternehmensberater:* management consultant; business consultant

The terms 'management counsellor' and 'business counsellor' –
which are given in some dictionaries – are rarely used. Counsellor
generally refers to a person who gives advice to people experiencing personal difficulties (e.g. the staff counsellor in US
organisations, the student counsellor or the marriage guidance
counsellor). In US English, a 'counsellor' may be an 'attorney' or
'lawyer'.

16   *verhindert dies, dass der häusliche Arbeiter sozial isoliert wird:*
this prevents the home worker from becoming socially isolated;
this stops the home worker from becoming socially isolated

Please note →

> Note that a gerund construction is needed in English.
> They could not prevent the firm from being taken over. *Sie
> konnten nicht verhindern, daß die Firma übernommen wurde.*

17   *(das) Bundesministerium (für):* (the) German ministry (of)
Strictly speaking, *Bundesministerium* is 'Federal Ministry', or, if it
is not clear from the context that you are referring to Germany,
'German Federal Ministry'. In practice, however, unless it is
important to emphasise that this is the 'German Federal Ministry',
(as opposed to, say, a 'regional ministry'), the form 'German
Ministry' is more likely to be used.

18   *statt nur zuhause zu arbeiten:* rather than working only at home;
rather than only working at home; instead of working only at
home; in preference to working only at home

Please note →

> Note the gerund constructions in the above options as well as
> the further examples of usage below.
> They would rather close the plant than give in to the union's
> demands. Rather than giving in to the union demands, they
> decided to close the plant. Would you like another drink? I'd
> rather not – I'm driving.

19   *hier muss nicht immer ein eigener zweiter Schreibtisch stehen:* a
second desk of one's own in the company is not always necessary;
it is not always necessary for the employee to have a second desk
of his or her own in the company
Examples of how to translate *'eine eigene'*, etc.
Sie hat eine eigene Wohnung: She has an apartment of her own.
Jugendliche sollten ein eigenes Konto haben. Young people ought
to have a bank account of their own/their own bank account.

20   *teilen einen Büroplatz:* share one office space; share the same
workstation; share one office area/desk

See also note [9] above.

[21] *Außendienstbeschäftigte:* travelling salesmen; (travelling) sales representatives; travelling salespeople; field sales staff/ personnel; sales staff in the field; sales reps (colloquial).

[22] *Wirtschaftsprüfer:* company auditors; auditors; external auditors; chartered accountants (GB); certified public accountants (US)

> ← Please note
>
> 'Auditors' *(Bilanzprüfer, Abschlussprüfer, Revisoren)* are people or firms appointed to carry out an audit *(Abschlussprüfung, Revision)* of an organisation. In the UK, external auditors must be members of a recognised body, such as the 'Institute of Chartered Accountants', in which case, they are called 'chartered accountants' *(öffentlich zugelassene Wirtschaftsprüfer)*. The equivalent US-term is 'certified public accountant (CPA)'.

[23] *Kunde:* client; customer

> ← Please note
>
> To some extent these two terms are interchangeable. In principle, both can refer to a person or a business that buys goods or services. A hairdresser, for example, has clients, a supermarket has customers, a bank has customers or clients.
> - 'Client': *Klient, Auftraggeber, Mandant*, is exclusively used when we refer to a person or business that uses the services of a professional (such as an accountant, consultant or lawyer).
> - 'Customer': *Kunde, Abnehmer*, is used for a person or business that orders/purchases something from a company. Related terms are
> buyer/purchaser: *Einkäufer, Käufer, Erwerber, Kunde*
> shopper: *Käufer, Kauflustiger*
> account: *Kunde, Kreditkunde* (i.e. a business or a trader that has an arrangement to buy from a particular supplier)
> key account: *Großkunde*
> fringe account: *Sekundärkunde*
> patron: *Gast, Stammkunde*, especially of a restaurant/hotel
> clientele: *Kundenkreis, Kundschaft, Klientel*

[24] *Auftrag:* commission; task; job; assignment
Cf. I.2.1, note [13], p. 14 and X.2.1, note [11], p. 137.

[25] *bündelt:* groups together; gathers together; brings together; collects together

Please note →

'Bundles (together)' seems inappropriate here, as 'to bundle' is often used when things are hastily and untidily gathered together.

Example

When the doorbell rang, he bundled all his dirty clothes into a cupboard.

However, 'bundle' is appropriate in some specific collocations, e.g. with words such as 'letters', 'packages', 'newspapers'.

Example

Bundle up the old newspapers and leave them outside the door.

In a business context, 'bundle' can mean to 'give away' or 'offer cheaply' one product related to another product being sold.

Example

The software packages are bundled with the hardware. *Software und Hardware werden als Komplettpaket angeboten.*

[26] *(Telearbeits-)Plätze:* telework spaces, telework desks, telework-stations

[27] *in der Nachbarschaft der Beschäftigten:* in the employees' neighbourhood; in the locality where the employees live; in the vicinity of the employees' homes

Please note →

- 'Neighbourhood' and 'vicinity' are not exact synonymous.

  Examples

  This is a pleasant neighbourhood.

  There are several hotels in the vicinity of London.

- Both expressions can be used in connection with a sum of money to indicate 'about', 'around', 'approximately'.

  Example

  We would expect an offer in the vicinity of/in the neighbourhood of $20,000.

- 'Proximity' is a (physical) closeness; the fact that a thing/a person is very close/near: *die unmittelbare Nähe, die allernächste Nähe*

  Example

  We are looking for premises which are in close proximity to the town centre.

[28] *diese Art der ausgelagerten Arbeit:* this type of work performed outside the company; this form of outwork; this form of telework

²⁹ *ist in Deutschland ... bislang jedoch kaum zu finden:* is, however, still very uncommon in Germany; is, however, still scarcely to be found in Germany

³⁰ *im Unterschied zu Großbritannien:* in contrast to Great Britain; unlike (in) Great Britain

← Please note

'In contrast to' and 'unlike' are best placed at the beginning or the end of a sentence or clause as they mark the contrast between the two elements they link. The expression 'in difference' does not exist.

Example

Im Gegensatz/Unterschied zu dir, muss ich auch an den Wochenenden arbeiten: Unlike you, I have to work at weekends too.

3.1 Terminology: workforce and work environment

III. 3 Exercises

1   Fill in the gaps by choosing the appropriate English equivalent of the German terms in (brackets). Use words and phrases from the sample translation and the notes. Note that there may be more than one option.

1   One advantage of telework is that it is possible for an organisation to recruit ___ *(Arbeitskräfte)* from all over the country, or even from all over the world.

2   Another advantage is that time-wasting and fuel-consuming commutes between the home and the ___ *(Arbeitsplatz)* become unnecessary.

3   Nowadays, she does much of her work from a ___ *(Arbeitsplatz)* in her home office.

4   Despite the increasing use of teleconferencing, face-to-face meetings on the company's ___ *(Räumlichkeiten)* still play an important role.

5   I have ___ *(unterschiedliche)* working hours every day.

6   Could you explain the ___ *(Unterschied)* between a blue and a white collar worker?

7   I'm working in my home office today, but I'll be ___ *(im Betrieb)* on Monday.

8   BGC Chemicals has set up a new ___ *(Betrieb)* in Malaysia for the production of softening agents.

9   In the current climate of recession, opening a new restaurant is a risky ___ *(Unterfangen/Unternehmen)*.

10 Animal rights protesters conducted a month-long campaign against the ___ *(Firma/Unternehmen)*, which specializes in drug-testing.

2 Using dictionaries, find the appropriate equivalent for the terms below. They are all related to the "place of work" and its environment.

Arbeitsmarkt	job market, labour market (US)
1 Arbeitsumgebung	____
2 Arbeitsleben	____
3 Arbeitserlaubnis	____
4 Datenverarbeitung	____
5 Datenschutz	____
6 Datenbank	____
7 Datenerfassung	____

8 Kundenverhalten
9 Kundendienst
10 Kundenkreis
11 Kundenbetreuung
12 Kundentreue
13 Stammkunde

14 Betriebsarzt	____
15 Betriebsbesichtigung	____
16 Betriebsferien	____
17 Betriebsausflug	____
18 Betriebsleiter	____
19 Büroausstattung	____
20 Bürobedarf	____
21 Büroräume	____
22 Bürogebäude	____
23 Bürozeit; auch: Büroöffnungszeiten	____

3.2 Tricky translations: words easily confused

1   Using dictionaries, provide an English definition and a German
    translation of the <u>underlined</u> words, which may easily be
    confused.
    1   <u>domestic</u> market
    2   <u>home</u> sales
    3   <u>domestic</u> appliances
    4   <u>home</u> computer
    5   her latest <u>enterprise</u> is an Internet gift shop
    6   the government is promoting <u>enterprise</u> in this region
    7   an economy based on <u>free enterprise</u>
    8   to create <u>jobs</u>
    9   to create a <u>workspace</u>
    10 safety in the <u>workplace</u>
    11 <u>consumer advice</u>
    12 <u>customer advice</u>
    13 to visit a <u>costumer</u>
    14 a population <u>in the vicinity of</u> 60,000,000
    15 <u>in the vicinity of</u> Düsseldorf's main station
    16 not a very reputable <u>neighbourhood</u>
    17 the <u>proximity</u> of my office to my home is a great advantage

2   Translate the following sentences. Include the suggestions made
    in (brackets).
    1   Dieses Seminar macht Sie mit wichtigen Verhandlungstechniken
        vertraut. (familiarise you/essential).
    2   Kommunikationstechnik muss heutzutage benutzerfreundlich
        sein.
    3   Der Kunde hat uns einen wichtigen Auftrag erteilt, der innerhalb
        der nächsten drei Wochen erledigt werden muss. (carried out/
        within)
    4   Das Firmengelände liegt in nächster Nähe zur Einkaufszone. (in
        close proximity; shopping precinct).
    5   Die Kaufsumme bewegt sich um die £5 Millionen. (vicinity)

3.3 Additional practice

1 *'Es gibt'* and similar constructions
Examples
Telework has actually existed for a long time.
It is a question of whether the money will be used for social reforms.
Four questions have to be answered.
It's a long way to Tipperary.

Please translate:
1 Es gibt vier Hauptformen der Telearbeit.
2 Internet-Reisebüros gibt es schon länger.
3 Es gab letztes Jahr einige Probleme mit den Lieferungen.
4 Es ging darum, ob die Regierung die Einnahmen dazu benutzen würde, das Haushaltsdefizit zu verringern.
5 Es sind noch einige Probleme zu lösen.
6 Zwischen 1994 und 2000 kam es zu einigen wichtigen Steuerreformen.
7 Es waren zehn Briefe zu beantworten.
8 Es wird in der Zukunft viele verschiedene Arbeitsformen geben.
9 Zum Flughafen sind es ungefähr zehn Kilometer.

2 The present perfect
Examples
Mobile telework has existed for a long time
We have had several changes of company structure since the merger.
What have you been doing since we last met?
I have not been to Australia recently.
Since obtaining that contract, we have been fairly optimistic.

Please translate:
1 Ich bin seit einiger Zeit unzufrieden mit seinen Leistungen.
2 Seit Juli schreiben wir schwarze Zahlen.
3 Seit der Fusion sind viele Arbeitsplätze verlorengegangen.
4 Was machen Sie eigentlich so in letzter Zeit?
5 Ich war neuerdings oft in London.
6 Seit sie sich um die Stelle beworben hat, hat sie nichts mehr gehört.
7 Seit die Firma übernommen wurde, gehen die Gewinne zurück.

IV   Intercultural Communication

IV Intercultural Communication

Im Geschäftsleben und überhaupt in allen praktischen Bereichen ist der Deutsche ein harter Gegner, wenn man mit ihm verhandelt. Er gibt nicht so leicht auf und nur im äußersten Notfall stimmt er Kompromissen zu. Er kennt keine noblen Gesten, ist weder großzügig noch ritterlich. Er ist der Meinung, dass kein Gewinn zu gering sein kann und dass es keine belanglosen Punkte gibt. Da in seinen Augen alles von Bedeutung ist, kämpft er auch um alles. Er macht keinerlei Zugeständnisse, es sei denn, es wäre in seinem Interesse. Er nutzt die geringste Schwäche, die kleinste Unaufmerksamkeit seines Gesprächspartners aus und teilt schamlos Tiefschläge aus. Wenn eine Vereinbarung über irgendein Detail nicht schriftlich festgelegt wurde, fühlt er sich nicht daran gebunden. Geschäfte werden zweifelsohne als Kampffeld angesehen, auf dem sich zwei Energien gegenüberstehen, von denen die stärkere den Sieg davonträgt. Aber wenn die Auseinandersetzung beendet ist, wird ihr Ausgang nicht mehr in Frage gestellt.

(Bernhard Nuss (1993:77), *Das Faust Syndrom. Ein Versuch über die Mentalität der Deutschen*, Bouvier Verlag, Berlin)

A tough cookie[1]

The German is a hard negotiation opponent both in business and **indeed**[2] in all practical areas of life. He does not give up so easily **and is only prepared to compromise in extreme cases**[3]. **He never makes any noble gestures**[4], and he is neither generous nor **chivalrous**[5].

He is of the opinion that no **gain**[6] can be too small and that there are no **trivial details**[7]. He fights for everything since, in his eyes, everything is of significance. He **makes no concessions**[8] whatsoever unless it is in his own interest to do so. He **takes advantage**[9] of the **tiniest sign of inattentiveness**[10] on the part of his business partner and **has no scruples about hitting below the belt**[11].

He does not feel duty-bound[12] **to abide by any agreed-upon detail**[13] which has not been **stipulated in writing**[14]. **There can be no doubt that**[15] **business transactions**[16] **are regarded as**[17] a battlefield where two powers confront each other and where only the stronger one will be victorious. However, once the conflict is ended, the outcome is no longer questioned.

2.1 Notes on the translation

[1] *ein harter Brocken:* a tough cookie; a tough nut to crack

> The metaphor 'a tough cookie' can only be used to characterize people. By contrast, 'a tough nut to crack' can be applied to both 'knotty problems' *(knifflige Probleme)* and 'difficult persons'.

← Please note

American saying:
When the going gets tough, the tough get going.

[2] *überhaupt:* indeed

> Note that negations and questions containing *überhaupt* can be translated as follows:
> *Geht das überhaupt?* Will this work at all?
> *Wir hatten überhaupt keine Informationen.* We had no information at all./We had no information whatsoever.

← Please note

[3] *und nur im äußersten Notfall stimmt er Kompromissen zu:* and is only prepared to compromise in extreme cases; and is only willing/ and only agrees to compromise in extreme cases

Please note →

Note that if the adverb 'only' is the first word of a sentence or clause, the subject and the verb of the main sentence have to be inverted.

Examples

... and only *(nur)* in extreme cases does he agree to (any) compromises.

Only after *(erst nachdem)* the deal had been signed, did the hostility die down.

For other aspects of 'only' see V.3.3, Additional practice, p. 75.

Idioms which also denote a compromise:

jemandem (auf halbem Wege) entgegenkommen: to meet somebody halfway

Konzessionen (Zugeständnisse) machen: to make concessions

einen Punkt zugestehen: to concede a point

nachgeben: to give way (on this point)

An 'uncompromising' attitude can be viewed as 'taking a tough stand' or as 'adopting a hard line'. 'Uncompromising' then corresponds to adamant, *unerbittlich, unnachgiebig, hart.*

Example

They remained adamant throughout the negotiations. *Während der ganzen Verhandlungen blieben sie hart.*

Please note →

Note also that 'to compromise' may signify 'to expose a person to disrepute': *jemanden kompromittieren.*

4   *er kennt keine noble Gesten:* he does not make noble gestures; he never makes noble gestures; he does not know the meaning of 'noble gestures'

German phrases such as *'Er kennt kein(e).../nichts als .../nur ...',* *'kennen'* cannot always be translated as 'to know'.

Examples

Er kennt keine Rücksichtnahme: He has no consideration for other people.

Sie kennen nichts als ihre Arbeit: They live for their work.

Er kennt keine Reue/kein Pflichtgefühl: He has no sense of remorse/no sense of duty.

5   *ritterlich:* chivalrous; gentlemanly

6   *Gewinn:* gain

> - 'Gain' is any advantage which is won, earned or – as in the text – otherwise acquired. Unlike 'profit', 'gain' is not necessarily of a financial nature.
> - 'Profit' is the monetary excess of revenues – arising from the sales of periodical outputs of products or services – over the full expense incurred by providing these outputs.

7 *belanglose Punkte:* trivial details, inconsequential issues, insignificant issues
Alternatively, this can be rendered as: 'details which are of no consequence/of no significance'.

8 *Zugeständnisse machen:* to make concessions; see note [3], p. 55.

9 *er nutzt ... aus:* he takes advantage of, he exploits, he makes use of

10 *die geringste Unaufmerksamkeit:* the tiniest sign of inattentiveness

Further example

Sie konnten nicht das geringste Anzeichen von Schwäche entdecken: They were unable to spot even the slightest sign of weakness.
The same message is contained in the metaphor:
They were unable to discover the smallest chink in his armour.
A 'chink' is a 'slight crack' in armour which, like an Achilles' heel, exposes the contestant in a fight or tournament to increased risks.
For further 'imperfections' *(Unzulänglichkeiten)*, 'weaknesses' *(Schwächen)* and 'deficiencies' *(Mängel)* see XI.2.1, note [28], p. 152.

11 *und teilt schamlos Tiefschläge aus:* and has no scruples about hitting below the belt, and is not ashamed to hit below the belt

12 *fühlt er sich nicht daran gebunden:* he does not feel duty-bound to abide by ; he does not feel honour-bound to abide by; he does not feel oblige/under any obligation to adhere to

> - 'Abide by' (rules, promises, agreements) corresponds to *sich an (Regeln, Versprechen, Vereinbarungen) halten.* Synonyms are 'stick to', 'adhere to' and 'observe'.
> - 'Be obliged', 'be obligated' (especially in US usage), 'be under an obligation' renders *verpflichtet sein/eine Verpflichtung eingegangen sein.*
> - 'Be honour-bound' and 'feel duty-bound' to do something express an ethical/moral obligation.

Please note →

> Note that 'be duty-bound' and 'be honour-bound' are usually followed by a verb.

¹³ *eine Vereinbarung über irgendein Detail:* any agreed-upon detail; any detail agreed on
For the collocations of 'agreement' see 3.1 Exercise 2, p. 59.

¹⁴ *schriftlich festgelegt:* stipulated in writing; laid down in writing; stated in written form

¹⁵ *zweifelsohne:* there can be no doubt that ...; without any doubt, ... it is an undisputed fact that ...; it is an incontrovertible fact that ...; no doubt ...
Some alternative translations of this sentence would be:
He obviously *(offensichtlich)* looks upon the market as a battlefield.
Business transactions are clearly regarded as a battlefield.

Further useful related expressions
When in doubt say nowt! (Yorkshire proverb): *Im Zweifelsfall sei lieber still.*
I am beginning to have my doubts about this project. *Mir kommen allmählich Zweifel an diesem Projekt.*
They are having second thoughts about the decision to hive off two core areas. *Sie zweifeln inzwischen an (der Richtigkeit der) Entscheidung, zwei Kernbereiche auszugründen.*
The evidence proved beyond a shadow of a doubt that she was innocent. *Die vorgelegten Beweise ließen nicht den geringsten Zweifel daran, dass sie unschuldig war.*

¹⁶ *Geschäfte:* business transactions, business deals, business
For the collocations and the grammatical intricacies of 'businesses' see X.3.3: Additional practice, p. 142.

¹⁷ *wird angesehen als:* is regarded as; is looked upon; is considered as; is considered to be; is thought to be; is assumed to be

Please note →

> Note that the auxiliaries *'sollen'* and *'wollen'* are frequently used when the above phrases are translated into German.
> Examples
> The German is thought to be/reputed to be an uncompromising/tough opponent. *Der Deutsche wird als kompromissloser Gegner angesehen./Man stellt sich den Deutschen als kompromisslosen Gegner vor./Der Deutsche soll ein kompromissloser Gegner sein.*

> He reckons he can manage that on his own. *Er glaubt, das alleine fertigzubringen. Er will das alleine können.*

3.1 Terminology: agreements

agree about • agree more • agreed with • agreed on • agreed to • as agreed • Is it agreed that ...

1 Please fill in the gaps. Use the box below to translate the expressions given in (brackets).

1 We could not ___ ! *(Wir sind ganz Ihrer Meinung!)*
2 The supplier has ___ the proposal made by the production manager. *(zugestimmt)*
3 In Germany, unions and shop owners never seem to ___ ___ shop opening hours. *(einer Meinung sein über)*
4 The following items were finally ___ . *(Übereinstimmung erzielen über ...)*
5 They all ___ ___ what was recommended in the report. *(stimmten zu)*
6 ___ we should ask for a second opinion? *(Sind alle der Meinung, dass ...)*
7 Can we take the following ___ ___ ? *(als vereinbart)*

2 Supply the English equivalent of these collocations with agreement.

eine Vereinbarung erzielen   to reach an agreement
1 eine V. anstreben   ___
2 eine V. treffen   ___
3 eine V. einhalten *(gesetzlich und ethisch)* ___
4 eine V. verletzen   ___
5 eine V. brechen   ___
6 eine V. umgehen   ___
7 eine V. widerrrufen   ___

3.2 Tricky translations

1 Metaphors and idioms
Translate the following sentences using the expressions supplied in the Notes on the translation.

1 Er war offensichtlich verhindert.
2 Da haben wir eine harte Nuss zu knacken.
3 Das war ein Schlag unter die Gürtellinie.
4 Wir sollten uns in der Mitte/auf halbem Weg treffen.
5 Die Firma fühlte sich verpflichtet, den Vertrag einzuhalten.
6 Die Kunden äußerten überhaupt keine Beschwerden (complaints).
7 Unsere Konkurrenz zeigte nicht die geringste Schwäche.
8 Sind Sie kompromissbereit?
9 Mir kommen Zweifel an dieser Entscheidung.
10 Er hielt unerbittlich an seiner Entscheidung fest.

2 Rumours and reputations
In English and German, there are a variety of expressions which refer to reputed, reported and rumoured activities. They may derive from
• our thoughts (thought to, considered to, assumed to)
• our perspective or view (regarded as, looked on as, held to be)
• hearsay (reputed to, said to, have the reputation of being, believed to, to be supposed to)
• our self-assessment (reckon).
For further grammatical and semantic aspects of 'should' see VI.3.3: Additional practice: Exercise 1: *Wie man 'sollte' übersetzen sollte*, p. 86.

Translate the sentences below into English.

1 Man hält ihn für pünktlich und tüchtig.
2 Unser Rivale gilt als fairer Gegner und das ist er auch.
3 Diese Aufgabe soll kinderleicht sein.
4 Die Firma ist dafür bekannt, dass sie hochwertige Ware liefert.
5 Er soll ein guter Kollege sein.
6 Er will ein guter Organisator sein.
7 Das Gepäck soll nach Paris gegangen sein.
8 Im allgemeinen glaubt man, dass Manager rational denken.
9 Er soll zugestimmt haben.

3.3 Additional practice: pinpointing the problem

Fill the gaps including the suggestions made below. All examples focus on the polysemous nature of *Punkt* and 'point'.

> bulletpoints • detail • dot • dotted line • full stop • no point in • in a nutshell • item • on the dot • period • point• point • point of • sharp • soft spot

1. To put the matter ___ ___ ___ *(auf den Punkt gebracht; langer Rede kurzer Sinn!)*, we are in favour of the project.
2. I would now like to move on to the next ___ on the agenda *(Tagesordnungspunkt)*.
3. Please complete your sentence by adding a ___ / ___ *(Punkt)*.
4. This information ought to be highlighted by ___ *(Auf-zählungszeichen)* in your CV.
5. The parcel will be delivered at 3 o'clock ___ /___ *(um Punkt drei)*.
6. ___ taken *(Das sehe ich ein)*!
7. This ___ is of no consequence *(Einzelheit; Einzelpunkt)*.
8. Our company turned over $4 million: four ___ six *(4,6)* to be precise.
9. Show me the ___ *(wo ich unterschreiben soll)*, I can't wait to sign this contract.
10. Proverb: There is no ___ ___ crying over spilt milk.
11. This student tends to ___ his i's and cross his t's *(er nimmt es zu genau)*.
12. Our Human Resources Manager has a ___ ___ *(Schwäche)* for cats.
13. Unfortunately, we seem to have reached the ___ ___ no return *(von hier gibt es kein Zurück)*.

V Management

V Management

Der Diskurs der modernen Managementtheorie geht davon aus, dass der Erfolg von Unternehmensstrategien ein logisches Ergebnis der systematischen Umsetzung überlegener Managementtechniken und kluger Entscheidungen von Führungskräften sei. Die Frage, wie und weshalb einige Unternehmen sich auszeichnen konnten, wo andere versagten, hat deshalb in den vergangenen beiden Jahrzehnten eine Reihe von Bestsellern hervorgebracht, die die Erfolgsrezepte der bestgeführten US Konzerne zu beschreiben suchten.

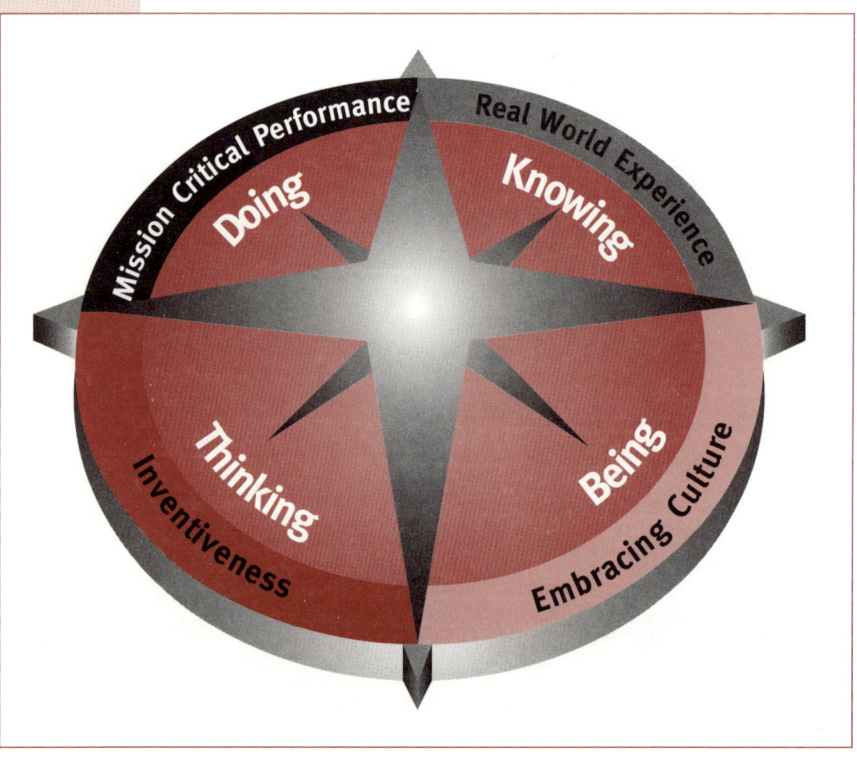

Eine der bekanntesten Veröffentlichungen auf diesem Gebiet ist der bereits 1982 erschienene Bestseller *Auf der Suche nach Spitzenleistungen*. Die Verfasser dieses Werkes, Tom Peters und Robert H. Waterman Jr. präsentierten eine Hitparade derjenigen Unternehmen die, gemessen an ihren Marktanteilen, als Sieger ihrer jeweiligen Branche hervorgegangen waren.

Sie empfahlen eine Reihe von goldenen Regeln, darunter
- die Verflachung hierarchischer Organisationsstrukturen
- die 'Verschlankung' der Mitarbeiter
- systemische Ansätze gerade in komplexen Unternehmensbereichen
- eine Unternehmenskultur, die von einem echten unternehmerischen Geist sowie von der Praxiserfahrung und der Wertorientierung der Führungskräfte geprägt ist
- die Konzentration auf Kernkompetenzen
- ungeteilte Loyalität gegenüber dem bestehenden Markt,
- Kundennähe sowie den Aufbau und die Pflege solider und tragfähiger Kundenbeziehungen.
- Nicht zuletzt sollen alle Mitarbeiter, Zulieferer und Kunden in die Entscheidungsprozesse und die strategische Zielsetzung des Unternehmens einbezogen werden.

Diese Ideen sprachen in erster Linie multinationale Groß- und Mischkonzerne an, ehe sie allmählich vom Mittelstand übernommen wurden. Also machten sich, angespornt von den leuchtenden nationalen Vorbildern, viele Führungskräfte auf die Suche nach unternehmerischer Perfektion und den vielgepriesenen Spitzenleistungen.

Auf Dauer zeigte sich jedoch, dass selbst Hochleister nicht immer dem Zahn der Zeit zu widerstehen vermögen: einige wurden, trotz ihrer Wettbewerbsstärke, von der Konkurrenz geschluckt, und andere überlebten nur, weil sie die Kostenvorteile von Skaleneffekten umsetzen konnten.

(M. Seidenspinner on: *In Search of Excellence*, T. J. Peters and Robert H. Waterman Junior, HarperCollins Publishers, Glasgow, 1982, repr. 1991)

In search of excellence[1]

The discourse of modern management theory **assumes**[2] the success of **corporate strategies**[3] to be a logical **outcome**[4] of the systematic **implementation**[5] of superior management techniques and of wise decisions made by **senior executives**[6]. Thus, **the question as to how and why**[7] some **companies**[8] have succeeded in achieving excellence where others have failed has, in the past two decades, **engendered**[9] a series of best-sellers, which have sought to describe the recipes for success of the ten best-run American **groups**[10].

One of the best-known publications in this area is *In Search of Excellence* which was published **as early as**[11] 1982. The authors of this work, Tom Peters and Robert H. Waterman Jr., presented a hit parade of those corporations which, measured in terms of their market **share**[12], had become champions **in their respective business sectors**[13]. They proposed **a series of**[14] golden rules such as

- **the delayering**[15] of hierarchical organisational structures
- **the downsizing of staff**[16]
- **systemic approaches**[17], especially in complex corporate areas
- a **corporate culture**[18] that is **moulded on**[19] a genuine entre-preneurial spirit as well as the **hands-on experience**[20] and value orientation of the corporation's senior management
- focussing on **core competencies**[21],
- **undivided allegiance**[22] to the existing market
- closeness to the customers as well as **forging and fostering**[23] sound and **sustainable**[24] customer relations.
- Last but not least, Peters and Waterman Jr. **suggest that all**[25] employees, suppliers and customers **should become integrated**[25] into corporate decision-making processes and in **defining the strategic goals**[26] of the organisation.

These ideas appealed, first and foremost, to major multinational **groups** and **conglomerates**[27], before being gradually adopted by **small and medium-sized enterprises**[28]. Thus, **motivated**[29] by the nation's shining examples, a good number of executives set out in search of entrepreneurial perfection and this **much vaunted**[30] excellence.

However, in the long run, it became evident that even high performers are not always **capable of**[31] standing the test of time: in spite of their **competitive edge**[32], some were **swallowed by their business rivals**[33], and others only survived due to their ability to realize the cost benefits achieved through **economies of scale**[34].

2.1 Notes on the translation

● ● ● ● ● ● ● ● ●

1 *Spitzenleistungen:* excellence; excellent performance; high performance

> *Spitzenleistungen* sums up a variety of high-level personal achievements.

2 *geht davon aus:* assumes; presupposes
3 *Unternehmensstrategien:* corporate strategies

← Please note

- 'Corporate' denotes everything pertaining to the company itself whereas 'entrepreneurial' is indicative of a personal attitude, namely that of a person endowed with 'busines acumen' *(Geschäftssinn)* who undertakes to provide an innovative product or service for a market.
- An 'entrepreneur' is a genuine risk taker who invests his/her own capital in a business and is prepared to face the consequences arising from this venture, hence 'entrepreneurship', 'entrepreneurism'. 'Entrepreneurial talent' is an important factor of production which impacts positively on national economic cycles.

4 *Ergebnis:* outcome; result
'Consequences' *(Folgen)* is a possible translation, too, although this may connote a negative outcome.
Examples
to suffer the consequences of one's folly: *die Konsequenzen seiner Torheit spüren*
to face the consequences arising from an investment: *den Folgen einer Investition ins Auge sehen*

5 *Umsetzung (Durchführung, Ausführung):* implementation; realization (esp. in US usage)
Examples
to implement a plan: *einen Plan verwirklichen*
to carry out a project: *ein Projekt durchführen*
to execute an order: *einen Auftrag ausführen*
to realize the benefits of economies of scale: *die Größenvorteile umsetzen*

6 *Führungskräfte:* senior executives; top executives; senior managers; senior management

Depending on the 'company's designation' *(Gesellschaftsform)*, its 'top management' includes:

Please note →

- 'Managing Director' ('MD'): In British-based organisations the 'MD' – also known as 'Chief Executive' – holds the highest ranking executive position and is directly accountable to the 'Board of Directors'. Within the US, 'Managing Director' is not an official occupational title listed by the Department of Labor. In some European subsidiaries of US corporation, however, the 'Managing Director' may be the legal head and the chief executive of the organisation. In these cases, he or she is directly accountable to the 'supervisory board' *(Aufsichtsrat)* of the subsidiary.
- 'Chief Executive Officer' ('CEO'): the highest ranking office within a US context, often combined with the position of company 'President' or that of a 'General Manager' *(Geschäftsführer)*. He/She is supported by one or more 'Chief Operating Officers' and/or 'Senior Vice-Presidents' and reports to the 'Board of Directors' which, according to W. Schäfer 'plays essentially the same advisory role' as the *Aufsichtsrat.*
- 'MDs', 'CEOs', 'Presidents' and 'General Managers' are responsible for planning, developing and implementing the corporate strategies which they align to the shared value systems of their organisations (see 'corporate culture' note [18], p. 71), the directives issued by the Board and the legal statutes that govern their type of corporation. They consult the senior executives, who are in charge of the most important corporate functions, in order to plan, co-ordinate and control all organisational activities which are instrumental in meeting the corporate goals.
- Certain functions inherent in the German 'two-tier system' *(Zweistufensystem)* of management and control – which includes labour representatives at both levels – have no equivalent in Anglo-American businesses. For this reason, a number of terms have been created (marked by an asterisk*)

to translate the German terminology. In an *Aktien-gesellschaft* (see III.2.1, note [14], p. 44, these management and supervisory structures are:

Vorstand: management board*/executive board*

Aufsichtsrat: supervisory board*

Vorstandsvorsitzende/r: chair(person) of the management board*

Aufsichtsratsvorsitzender: chair(person) of the supervisory board*

Arbeitsdirektor: executive for labour relations*

Hauptversammlung: shareholders' meeting/stockholders' meeting/general meeting

In German private limited companies (see III.2.1, note [14], p. 44.), the tasks of the *Geschäftsführer* correspond to those of a 'General Manager' (US), 'Director' or 'Managing Director'. The counterpart of the *Vorsitzende/r* or the *Leiter/in der Geschäftsführung* is again the 'CEO' or the 'Managing Director'. The *GmbH* may also have an *Verwaltungsrat:* 'administrative board' or an optional advisory board.

The *Beirat* or 'advisory board' is an optional function which exists in both Anglo-American and German companies.

7   *die Frage, wie und weshalb:* the question as to how and why

← Please note

Especially in British English, 'as to' may be used instead of 'about' or 'of'. 'As to' is usually followed by a 'wh-word'.

Examples

The discussion about / as to whether we should go ahead with our plan was postponed. *Die Diskussion (darüber), ob wir unseren Plan fortführen sollten, wurde verschoben.*

The question of/as to who ought to be invited was openly discussed. *Die Frage, wer eingeladen werden sollte, wurde offen diskutiert.*

8   *Unternehmen:* companies
For detailed definitions of business organisations see III.2.1, note [14], p. 44.

9   *hervorgebracht:* engendered; given rise to

10   *Konzerne:* groups, major corporations

← Please note

'Concern' is semantically complex. It can mean 'business', as in: 'They own a going concern': *Sie besitzen ein gutgehendes,*

•••••••• *Gewinn abwerfendes Geschäft.* However, US business periodicals use 'concern' occasionally when they make reference to a 'major corporation'.

For further denotations of 'concern' see VI.2.1, note [25], p. 84 and XI.2.1, note [5], p. 149.

[11] *bereits:* as early as; as far back as
For additional practice on *schon* and *erst* see .3.3, p. 75.

[12] *Marktanteil(e):* market share

Please note →

A 'market share' (singular noun form) is the percentage held by a corporation in its current market.

[13] *in ihrer jeweiligen Branche:* in their respective business sector; in their respective branch of industry

Please note →

A 'branch' is an office or shop that is part of a large organisation, especially in retailing or banking *(Niederlassung, Filiale, Zweigstelle, Geschäftsstelle).* 'Industry' is also a common translation of *Branche (d.h. Wirtschaftszweig, Industriezweig),* especially in compounds, as in 'the automotive industry'.
'Branch' may be considered a false friend, as it does not, by itself, translate *Branche.*

[14] *eine Reihe von:* a series of; a number of
'Series' can be a deceptive. It must not be mistaken for a plural form.
For further practice on singular and plural forms see II.3.3, Exercise 2, p. 37.

[15] *Verflachung:* delayering

Please note →

'Delayering' stands for the removal of hierarchical corporate 'layers' in order to achieve a higher degree of flexibility and customer closeness. Facilitated by the introduction of management information systems, and by innovative HRM strategies, such as staff 'empowerment' (see VII.2.1, note [25], p. 98), it has particularly affected middle management positions.

[16] *Verschlankung der Mitarbeiter:* the downsizing of staff; lean staff

Please note →

'Downsizing' (in colloquial American usage 'rightsizing') is the reduction in size of parts of an organisation in order to save costs and/or to increase productivity. The expected outcome is that of a 'leaner' *(schlanker),* more efficient and more profitable organisation.

'Downsizing measures' mostly affect the payroll staff, but also the management (see note [15]) and non-core operational units.

[17] *systemische Ansätze:* systemic approaches; systems approaches

← Please note

'Systems approaches' view organisations and their complex microcosms as living organisms. Rather than analysing the individual units of a company, 'systems thinking' explores the relationships and the interaction between the various layers and compartments. It rejects the traditional formal planning and control approach with its single focus (one vision, limited core skills and linear control) as inadequate.

[18] *Unternehmenskultur:* corporate culture

← Please note

'Corporate culture' is the system of shared values that provides and sustains 'meaning' in a corporation. It is founded on an internal web – also known as 'paradigm' *(Paradigma)* – of norms, beliefs, traditions, legends, myths and rites, etc. as well as on the symbols (logo, slogans) and messages (vision statement, strategic focus) which are communicated by the company to its external environment.

[19] *von ... geprägt:* moulded on; shaped by
[20] *Praxiserfahrung:* hands-on experience; first-hand knowledge

← Please note

The direct exposure of chief executives to the shopfloor is 'learning by doing' (a phrase coined in the 1950s by John Dewey), as opposed to the 'let's apply theory to practice' approach. It is also referred to as 'on-the-job training' or 'action learning'.
In CVs *Praxiserfahrung* is best translated as 'vocational experience' *(berufliche Erfahrung)*. Students are advised to avoid the rendering 'practical' as this often refers to low-level manual activities.

Related expressions
Management in practice: *Management in der (betrieblichen) Praxis*
This is good/best practice in our business sector: *Das ist eine bewährte/beispielhafte Vorgehensweise in unserer Branche.*
Managers are expected to practise what they preach: *Man erwartet von Managern, dass sie ihren Worten Taten folgen lassen.*
Practice makes perfect. *Übung macht den Meister.*

●●●●●●●●   [21] *Kernkompetenzen:* core competencies/ competences; core skills; key competencies

Please note →

> 'Core competencies' *(Kern- oder Schlüsselkompetenzen)* are the distinctive skills (e.g. technological know-how, patents, specialist expertise) that sustain a company's 'core business' *(Kerngeschäft)* and its 'key business areas' *(Hauptgeschäfts-bereiche)*. 'Core competencies' are of strategic importance: they contribute to the competitive edge of a company.
>
> Peters and Waterman Jr. recommend in this context that companies ought to 'stick to their knitting' (p. 292-305). This can be translated as: *Schuster bleib bei deinen Leisten.*

[22] *ungeteilte Loyalität:* undivided allegiance; undivided loyalty

[23] *Aufbau und Pflege:* forging and fostering; building and nurturing

[24] *tragfähig:* sustainable

'Sustainable' signifies 'capable of being maintained at a steady level'. In economics, it translates *'nachhaltig'*, as in 'sustainable development' *(nachhaltige Entwicklung)*.

[25] *sollen alle einbezogen werden:* they suggest that all ... should become integrated

'Sollen' here states what Peters and Waterman suggest that companies should do and this has to be made clear in the translation. For more details on how to translate *sollen* see VI.3.3 Additional practice: Meeting expectations, p. 88.

[26] *strategische Zielsetzung:* defining the strategic goals; setting the strategic directions

Please note →

> As business terms, 'goal', 'objective' and 'target' have specific meanings:
> - *allgemeine, übergeordnete Ziele:* goals; aims and objectives
>   In the course of strategy formation, companies determine their super-ordinate 'goals' which comprise all their general 'aims' (qualitative) and their detailed 'objectives' (quantitative). These have to be aligned with the overall corporate strategy and the available human and financial resources.
> - *konkrete Zielvorgaben:* objectives: i.e. quantifiable or quantified aims, e.g. an increase in market share of 20 percent.
> - *spezifische Planziele:* targets
>   Targets are precisely defined, time-related objectives in specific business areas, especially in sales and production. See also 3.1: Exercise 2: Aims and objectives, p. 74.

²⁷ *Groß- und Mischkonzerne:* major groups and conglomerates
Conglomerates are diverse groups of largely independent firms
generally managed by a holding company.

²⁸ *Mittelstand, mittelständische Unternehmen (KMU):* small and
medium-sized enterprises (SME); small and mid-sized businesses
(US)

> The English acronym 'SME' has found its linguistic counterpart
> in KMU which stands for *kleine und mittelständische Unter-*
> *nehmen.*
> In English business texts, 'mittelstand' is used as a neologism.

← Please note

²⁹ *angespornt:* motivated; inspired
³⁰ *vielgepriesen:* much vaunted; highly acclaimed
³¹ *vermögen:* to be capable of; to be in a position to; to be able to
³² *Wettbewerbsstärke:* competitive edge, competitiveness
³³ *von der Konkurrenz geschluckt:* swallowed by their business
rivals,; gobbled up by their business opponents/by the competition

> *Konkurrenz* makes reference to the fact that there is
> 'competition' and 'rivalry' *(Wettbewerb, Wettkampf)* in the
> marketplace and also to the active 'contestants' or
> 'competitors' *(Wettbewerber, Konkurrenten).*

← Please note

³⁴ *Skaleneffekte:* economies of scale; scale effects
'Economies of scale' *(Skaleneffekte, Größenvorteile, Größen-*
degression) signifies the reduction in unit costs as a result of
increased production output, large-scale operations and/or 'global
sourcing' *(globale Akquisition/Beschaffung).*

3.1 Terminology

1 Competition and competitors

Fill in the gaps by choosing the appropriate term from the box below.

achieved • acquired a reputation • credited • competitors • competitive advantages • competitiveness • conglomerate • decrease • economies of scale • effect • emulation • entrepreneurs • factors of production • labour costs • location • occur • reduction • referred to • rival • SME • unit costs

1   The fact that companies frequently copy successful product ideas from their major ___ (Konkurrenz, Konkurrenten) is sometimes ___ (bezeichnet) as ___ (Emulierung).

2   ___ (Größenvorteile) are intended to effect a ___ / ___ (Senkung) in ___ (Stückkosten).

3   On the one hand, this can be ___ (erreicht) internally by making more efficient use of the ___ ___ ___ (Produktionsfaktoren), on the other, this can be caused externally by lower ___ ___ (Lohnkosten) or other ___ ___ (Wettbewerbsvorteile) which determine the suitability of a business ___ (Standort).

4   SAP used to be a typical German ___ (mittelständisches Unternehmen) whereas ABB has ___ ___ ___ (sich den Ruf erworben) of being a genuine ___ (Mischkonzern) as well as a global player.

5   Richard Branson is generally ___ (anerkannt) with being one of the outstanding ___ (Unternehmer) of our time.

6   He continually seeks to improve the ___ (Wettbewerbsfähigkeit) of his companies.

2 Aims and objectives

Fill in the gaps using your dictionaries and the terminology provided in the notes.

1   The company has reason to be satisfied with their financial ___ (Ergebnisse). The sales staff have not only ___ (erfüllten) their ___ ___ (Verkaufsziele) but actually ___ (übertrafen) them.

2   One of the ___ (spezifische Ziele) determined by the marketing department was to ___ (ausweiten) the existing market base by defeating the new market challenger.

3   The predominant ___ (Ziel) of our supplier was to ___ ___ (umsetzen) the ISO 9000 quality standards by the end of the year.

4   ___ *(Entwicklungshilfe)* ___ *(zielt darauf ab)* to enable low income
    countries to ___ *(aufrechterhalten)* a steady level of economic
    improvement without ___ *(erschöpfen)* their natural resources or
    destroying their environment.
5   English proverb: ___ *(Erfolg)* has many fathers but ___ *(Mißerfolg)*
    is an orphan.

3.2 Tricky translations

Translate the sentences below using the terms provided in the notes.

1   Größenvorteile sollen zu einer Senkung der Stückkosten führen.
2   Kernkompetenzen sind von strategischer Bedeutung für jedes
    Unternehmen.
3   Das ist ein beispielhaftes Verfahren in der holzverarbeitenden
    Industrie.
4   Erfolgreiche Manager müssen Praxiserfahrung haben, Spitzen-
    leistungen erbringen und mit gutem Beispiel vorangehen.
5   Die Firma braucht einen Paradigmawechsel.
6   Der deutsche Mittelstand genießt weltweit den Ruf, besonders
    wettbewerbsstark zu sein.
7   Wie kann der „Standort Deutschland" wieder attraktiver werden?
8   Die richtige Unternehmenskultur soll die Mitarbeitermotivation
    erhöhen und die Identifizierung mit dem Unternehmen erleichtern.
9   Der systemische Ansatz ist mit der Chaostheorie verwandt.

3.3 Additional practice: *schon, nur, erst*

These adverbs are grammatically multifunctional and semantically
complex. The following exercise is intended to offer some guidance
which will assist the learner in making an informed choice when
rendering these adverbs into English.

*   *schon, bereits:* as impletives (i.e. semantic 'fillers'): no translation
    In combinations such as *schon immer, schon viele Jahre, bereits*
    and *schon* are not translated into English as their semantic
    reference is included in the present perfect tense. In the sentences
    below, it would even sound odd if 'already' (which is the trans-
    lation mostly attempted) were added to the English sentences.
    Examples
    I have known this for years. *Das weiß ich schon seit Jahren.*
    We have often asked them not to interfere: *Wir haben ihnen schon
    oft gesagt, dass sie sich nicht einmischen sollen.*

This process was completed yesterday./The process was already completed yesterday (US). *Der Vorgang ist bereits seit gestern abgeschlossen.*

- schon: affirmative adverb
  Das wird schon klappen. It'll all work out in the end. It will work out one way or the other/somehow.
- *bereits/schon* (referring to the past): as early as/as far back as
  Das war schon in den 50er Jahren bekannt. This was well known as far back as the 50s.
- *erst:* not before, not until
  Sie können uns erst um 3 Uhr erreichen (nicht vor 3 Uhr). You cannot contact us before 3 o'clock. You will not be able to reach us until three.
- *nur:* only
  Der Vertreter ist nur heute im Haus. (nicht gestern und auch nicht morgen).
  The sales representative is only in today.

Translate the following sentences into English.
1 Wie lange haben Sie schon Kenntnis davon?
2 Die Sitzung beginnt erst um 14:50.
3 Dies ist schon das dritte Mal, dass er heute anruft.
4 Erst seit dem frühen 20. Jahrhundert nutzt die Industrie die Vorteile der Automatisierung.
5 Das ist schon seit Jahren das Motto unserer Firma.
6 Unser Abteilungsleiter macht das schon.
7 Dieser Film wird nur heute gezeigt.
8 Um diese Frage wird man sich erst später kümmern können.

VI Leadership Culture

VI Leadership Culture

Fairness und Offenheit

Die Qualität der Mitarbeiterführung wird zunehmend zum entscheidenden Faktor für den Unternehmenserfolg. Doch was zeichnet gute Führung aus? Rolf Schwaneberg fasst es so zusammen: „Eine Führungskraft muss gemeinsam mit den Mitarbeitern die Ziele und Interessen des Unternehmens verfolgen und dabei deren persönliche Entwicklung im Blick behalten. Sie sollte die Mitarbeiterführung als wesentlichen Teil ihrer Aufgabenstellung verstehen und als persönlichen Erfolgsfaktor nutzen." Inwieweit dies gelinge, hänge wesentlich vom Selbstverständnis und Engagement des einzelnen Managers ab.

Wertschätzung, Wertschöpfung und Wegweiser

Im Ergebnis, so die Vision des Bereichs, soll sichergestellt sein, dass

- alle Telekom-Führungskräfte den ihnen anvertrauten Mitarbeitern Wertschätzung entgegenbringen,
- sie durch wertorientiertes Führen Wertschöpfung erzielen und
- alle Mitarbeiter des Konzerns die Personalführung und -entwicklung als konstanten Orientierungsrahmen im Wandel wahrnehmen.

„Führen bei der Telekom bedeutet, ganzheitlich und bereichsübergreifend im Interesse des Unternehmens zu denken und zu handeln sowie die Mitarbeiter zu fordern und zu fördern", definiert Schwaneberg den Auftrag des Managements. „Vor allem in Zeiten ständiger Veränderungen ist es von essentieller Bedeutung, ein motivierendes Arbeitsumfeld und -klima zu schaffen, Ängste frühzeitig abzubauen und eine vertrauensvolle Zusammenarbeit zu gewährleisten."

(*Zur Führungskultur bei der Deutschen Telekom*/Deutsche Telekom AG/E-Mail: DT_Vision@t-online.de)

On the leadership culture[1] of the Deutsche Telekom
Fairness and Openness

The quality of an organisation's **human resource management**[2] is increasingly becoming the **crucial**[3] factor in its commercial success. But **what are the distinguishing features of good leadership**[4]? Rolf Schwaneberg sums it up as follows: **senior executives have to pursue the goals**[5] and interests of their organisation together with the employees **while considering the personal development of the latter**[6]. **Managers should perceive HRM**[7] as an essential element **of the tasks assigned to them**[8] and should use it as a means of achieving personal success. To what extent they succeed – or not – **essentially**[9] depends on **how each manager conceives of his/her role**[10] and on the degree of his/her **commitment**[11].

Recognizing Value[12], Adding Value[13] and Setting Directions[14]

According to the **vision statement**[15] of this **section**[16] **the following outcome is to be attained**[17].

* All Telekom executives are expected to recognize the value of the performance of the employees entrusted to them.
* Added value is to be achieved by **value-oriented**[18] leadership
* All employees of the organisation are to perceive HRM and Personnel Development as a permanent **frame of reference**[19] for organisational change.

Consequently, Schwaneberg defines the managerial task as follows: "Leadership at Telekom signifies the pursuit of the interests of the enterprise by thinking and acting in a **holistic**[20], **cross-departmental**[21] manner and **by presenting a challenge to the staff and by promoting their development**[22]."

Especially in times of constant change, it is **vitally important**[23] to create a motivating work environment and **atmosphere**[24] **to allay (employee) concerns**[25] at an early stage and to warrant co-operation which is **governed by trust**[26].

●●●●●●●● **2.1 Notes on the translation**

Please note →

1   *Führungskultur:* leadership culture

- *Führung* i.e. 'management', 'governance', comprises firstly, all the functions and tasks performed by the executives *(Führungsaufgaben, Leitungsaufgaben)* of a company. If these tasks are allocated to specific 'departments' or 'units' the person in charge is referred to as *Leiter*.
  Examples
  Abteilungsleiter: head of department
  Produktionsleiter: production manager
- Secondly, *Führung* implies the talent for 'leadership' which encompasses the qualities and skills of a leader capable of 'walking the talk', i.e. of incorporating and representing the company's shared value system (see V.2.1, note [18], p. 71).
- Whereas modern management that predominantly focuses on the functional organisation (see IX.2.1, note [7], p. 123) closely associates leadership with the 'chain of governance' *(Führungsstruktur, Kontrollstruktur)* and with the idea of dominance, power and control, in the postmodern enterprises of the IT era, 'leadership' is defined as the quality to achieve excellent performance by motivating people, by managing complexity and change, by benefiting from conflict and – this is the most difficult task for 'modern' managers – by challenging their own favourite assumptions. See also V.2.1, note [6], p. 67, for *Führungskräfte*.

2   *Mitarbeiterführung:* Human Resource(s) Management; HRM, people management; also: 'leadership'

Please note →

In the wake of the 'Total Quality Management Movement', the large majority of corporations developed a distinct employee focus in the 1980s which gave rise to the strategically-oriented 'Human Resources Management' whose aims are mirrored in the Telekom text. 'People management' is gradually replacing the traditional 'personnel management' *(Personalwesen)* approach which had previously concentrated on the selection of staff and the control of labour costs.

3   *entscheidend:* crucial, decisive
4   *Was zeichnet gute Führung aus?:* What are the distinguishing features of a good leadership? What are the distinguishing traits/characteristics of good leadership?

5 *eine Führungskraft muss die Ziele ... verfolgen:* senior executives have to pursue the goals
For detailed definitions of *'Ziele'* see V.2.1, note [26], p. 72; for *'Führungskraft'* see V.2.1, note [6], p. 67.

> Gender-bias in favour of the all-pervasive male forms can be avoided by using plural nouns in the English version.

← Please note

6 *und dabei deren persönliche Entwicklung im Blick haben:* while considering the personal development of the latter; while taking the personal development of their staff into account/into consideration

> It is more reader-friendly to translate the definite article *deren* as 'of the latter' (i.e. *der letzteren*).
> The personal pronoun 'their' would be confusing here as this might be a pro form for 'senior executives' as well as for 'goals and interests'.

← Please note

7 *sie sollten Mitarbeiterführung verstehen als:* managers should perceive HRM as; leaders ought to regard/define people management as; the former ought to realize/comprehend/ understand that HRM represents

> It is necessary to replace the personal pronoun *'sie'* by 'managers' or 'the former'; the personal pronoun 'they' would be confusing as it could represent either 'managers' or 'employees'.

← Please note

See VIII.2.1, note [5], p. 108 for further translations of *'verstehen'*.

8 *ihrer Aufgabenstellung:* of the tasks assigned to them; of the tasks allocated to them; of their specific tasks

9 *wesentlich:* essentially; largely

10 *Selbstverständnis:* how each manager conceives of his/her role; how each individual defines his or her function and responsibilities

11 *Engagement:* commitment, personal involvement

12 *Wertschätzung:* recognizing value, appreciating value; value recognition also; value appraisal

> *Wertschätzen/einer Leistung Wert beimessen* is a semantically complex entity which finds its closest equivalent in 'recognition', and 'appreciation'.

← Please note

Wertschätzung literally means 'to assess the value of members of staff and/or of their performance': *den Wert (einer Person, einer Leistung) bemessen/einschätzen.* This type of evaluation, assessment or appraisal is carried out on an annual basis. It is predominantly founded on quantitative crtiteria such as the number of responsibilities allocated, the workload, the amount and the quality of work produced etc.

Telekom, however, emphasises the qualitative element of the valuing process which connotes the 'recognition of an employee's performance'.

Example

He was awarded a medal in recognition of his services.

The following verbs express the semantic dualism contained in *wertschätzen* vs. *den Wert schätzen:*

- *bewerten/bemessen* (quantitative): to appraise, to evaluate, to assess, to rate (i.e. to establish an order of excellence), to accredit (to apply an accreditation system/a credit system)
- *anerkennen/wertschätzen/Wert beimessen* (qualitative): to recognize, to value, to appreciate, to acknowledge, to credit somebody with ...

[13] *Wertschöpfung:* adding value; value adding

Please note →

'Value adding' is the additional value that is placed on a product as it passes the manifold stages of its development. The whole enhancement process is described as the 'value chain' *(Wertschöpfungskette).* 'Value adding' also applies to the development of services.

[14] *Wegweiser:* setting directions; direction setting

Please note →

Strictly speaking, *Wegweiser* signifies 'signpost' or – in loose usage – a person who gives directions or offers guidance.

For stylistic reasons, the translation offered here focuses on the 'tasks of a senior manager' rather than picturing him as a 'signpost'.

[15] *Vision:* vision, vision statement; mission statement; statement of strategic intent

Please note →

A 'vision statement' is issued by all major companies as an expression of their principal ethical orientation, general purpose and strategic direction. Such statements are shaped and guided by the type of corporate governance, stakeholder expectations, business ethics and the cultural context pertaining to a corporation. 'Vision statements' outline the *raison d'être* for both the management and the staff of an enterprise as well as for its external stakeholders.

The 'stakeholders' *(Interessengruppen)* are those persons or organisations that have a vested interest in a company. They comprise – *inter alia* – customers, staff, suppliers, shareholders, local authorities and consumer groups.

[16] *Bereich:* section; area; division
The 'section' referred to here is Human Resources.

[17] *im Ergebnis soll sichergestellt sein, dass:* the following outcome is to be attained; the following outcome is to be achieved

← Please note

> '*Im Ergebnis soll sichergestellt sein*' has to be rephrased as *dieses Ergebnis soll (ganz bestimmt) erreicht werden* in order to make this sentence easier to translate.
> 'Safeguard' would not be correct here. For its specific meaning see I.2.1., note [25], p. 17.

For further translations of *Ergebnis* see V.2.1, note [4], p. 67.

[18] *wertorientiert:* value-oriented; guided by values; value-led; value-driven

← Please note

> 'Value-oriented management' is an important recent development in management theory. It has gradually supplemented the former 'management by objectives' approach which encouraged all management levels to set quantitative objectives against which the corporate, divisional, departmental or individual performance was then assessed.

[19] *konstanter Orientierungsrahmen:* permanent frame of reference; constant frame of reference

[20] *ganzheitlich:* holistic
'Holistic' approaches comprehend organisations as a whole (similar to a living organism) rather than seeing them as a sum of individual organisational constituents. They are related to 'systems thinking' (see: V.2.1, note [17], p. 71).

[21] *bereichsübergreifend:* cross-departmental; multi-functional

← Please note

> 'Cross-departmental interaction' seeks to ensure the free flow of ideas and information within a company. It aims at 'cross-fertilisation' *(gegenseitige Befruchtung)* and seeks to pool

●●●●●●●● synergies and to break down the 'rigid compartmentalisation' (*Schubkastenaufteilung*) of more traditional organisations.

22 *fordern und fördern:* by presenting a challenge to the staff as well as by promoting their development
Both verbs are difficult to translate. *Gefordert sein* signifies 'to be confronted/faced with a difficulty or challenge'. *Fördern* indicates that someone is 'being encouraged, supported or promoted'.

Examples
Ausbildungsförderung: study grant
Familienförderung: family support scheme
Jugendförderung: Youth Opportunity Programme
Mitarbeiterförderung: employee development, staff development, personnel development

23 *essentiell:* vitally important; crucial; essential
24 *Klima:* atmosphere; climate
25 *Ängste abbauen:* to allay employee concerns; to sooth employee fears

Examples
The Sales Manager expressed his concern about the decreasing turnover. *Der Verkaufsleiter brachte seine Besorgnis wegen des rückläufigen Verkaufsumsatzes zum Ausdruck.*
This is the least of our concerns/worries. *Das ist unsere geringste Sorge.*
For further aspects of 'concern' see V.2.1, note [10], p. 69 (*Geschäft*), and XI.1.2, note [5], p. 149 (*betreffen*).

26 *vertrauensvoll:* governed by trust; characterized/guided by trust

VI.3 Exercises

3.1 Terminology: values and evaluation
Fill in the gaps. Most terms required can be taken from the notes above.

1 Each self-respecting company nowadays feels obliged to ___ (*veröffentlichen*) a ___ ___ (*Vision*) which outlines its shared ___ (*Werte*) and how it ___ (*wahrnehmen*) itself as part of its business environment.

2 Customers and employees ought to scrutinize each vision statement and ___ / ___ (*bewerten*) its genuineness. The proof of the pudding is, after all, in the eating.

3 Up-to-date ___ ___ ___ (*Mitarbeiterführung*) aims at ___ (*Mitarbeiter-*) motivation and consistent methods of ___ ___ (*Leistungsbewertung*).

4   ___ / ___ *(wertorientiertes)* management is a recent development **Exercises**
in corporate life. It has been an ___ *(wesentlich)* addition to
modern management which tended to rely exclusively on ___ ___
(quantitative Zielvorgaben) and often neglected the 'soft' issues
such as the ___ ___ *(Humanfaktor)* and the existing ___ ___
(Unternehmenskultur).

5   Most ___ *(Führungskräfte)* seek to eradicate the rigid ___
(Schubkastenmentalität) which absorbs a huge amount of their
company's energy and time.

6   However, the easy ___ *(Zugang)* to relevant information, the free
___ ___ ___ / ___ ___ *(Wissenstransfer)* and the ___ ___ *(Syner-
gieeffekte)* the management hoped for have not always
materialized.

7   Training forms an important part of ___ *(Personalentwicklung).*

8   Jack Welch, the erstwhile president of GE, ___ *(prägte)* the
proverbial phrase that 'a manager must walk the talk', in other
words he must ___ ___ ___ ___ *(den Worten Taten folgen lassen).*

3.2 Tricky translations
Example
*Ein guter Mitarbeiterführer sollte Konflikte weitmöglichst positiv
sehen; denn dies könnte entscheidend dazu beitragen, das Arbeits-
klima zu verbessern.* A good leader ought to go as far as possible
towards viewing conflicts in a positive light, as this might be
instrumental in improving the work atmosphere.

Translate the following sentences using one of the following
expressions which have to be embedded in a gerund structure.

> *an etwas denken:* consider
> *darauf abzielen, auf etwas aus sein:* to aim at
> *die Aussicht darauf:* the prospect of
> *entschlossen sein:* to be intent on
> *wenn es darum geht:* when it comes to
> *es schaffen:* succeed in
> *Freude haben an:* enjoy
> *es ist es nicht wert:* it is not worth
> *sich engagieren für:* to be committed to
> *an etwas hindern:* prevent from
> *in der Absicht:* with a view to

1 Ich ging zum Reisebüro in der Absicht, einen Flug nach Japan zu buchen.

2 Der Personalchef war entschlossen, eine leistungsgerechte Bezahlung einzuführen.

3 Der Geschäftsführer engagierte sich dafür, dass alle Führungskräfte sich der Werkspraxis aussetzten.

4 Hast du ernsthaft daran gedacht, diesen Prozess zu verbessern?

5 Ein Ziel ist es nicht wert, erreicht zu werden, wenn der Weg dorthin keinen Spaß macht.

6 Die Aussicht darauf, kritisiert zu werden, hindert viele daran, ihre Meinung zu sagen.

7 Personalentwicklungsprogramme zielen darauf ab, dem Unternehmen erfahrene und engagierte Mitarbeiter zu erhalten.

8 Die Firma hat es geschafft, einen Leistungsindex als festen Bestandteil der Mitarbeiterführung zu etablieren.

9 Wenn es darum geht, langfristige Bündnisse mit Kunden zu entwickeln, ist die Sprachkompetenz oft ein entscheidender Faktor.

3.3 Additional practice

1 *Wie man "sollte" übersetzen sollte.*

One of the previous chapters dealt with the present tense of the auxiliary *sollen* which is a helpful structure when translating rumours and assumptions (see IV.3.2, Exercise 2, p. 60). The following exercises focus on *sollte/n* as a past and a conditional form of *sollen*, which possess their own share of semantic complexity.

• the past form of *sollen*: *Sollte/n* – like the synonymous expression *hätte sollen* – represents the past tense of *sollen*:
Sollten Sie diese Aufgabe nicht gestern erledigen? Hätten Sie diese Aufgabe nicht gestern erledigen sollen?
Weren't you supposed to accomplish this task yesterday?

• the conditional form of *sollen*: *Sollte/n* refers to a potential, often future-based activity. This type often contains a recommendation:
Vielleicht sollten Sie sich alles noch einmal ansehen, ehe Sie eine Verpflichtung eingehen. Maybe you should review the situation, before committing yourself.

The homonymic clash between the past and the conditional forms in German creates a translation problem. Whereas the auxiliaries *können*, *müssen*, *dürfen* employ the *Umlaut* to highlight the difference between the past tense *(konnte, musste, durfte)* and the conditional (*könnte, müsste dürfte*), the simple past and the conditional of *sollen* and *wollen* sound like the same grammatical tense and are therefore easily confused.

The following example serves as a case in point.
Warum sollte ich Sie (gestern) anrufen?
1   Why did you want me/was I supposed to phone you yesterday?
2   Why should I phone you?
Whereas the speaker of sentence 1 simply wants to know factually why he was expected to call somebody, the second speaker expresses his reluctance to make a phone call in the first place. This may even be misunderstood as 'I do not phone people like you!' and thus cause embarrassment or offense.

The exercises below illustrate the difference between the two tenses.
1   It was supposed to happen
    The all-inclusive – rather formal – translation of the past form *ich sollte* is 'I was to'. But depending on the particular information one wishes to convey, there are a number of options which cover a variety of semantic nuances and allow us to fine-tune our message. The most frequently used of these options are listed in the central column of the box below.

to be	supposed	to
	expected	
	meant/intended	
	asked/requested/told	
	recommended/invited	
	destined	

Now consider the possible interpretations of the following sentences and translate them accordingly.
1   Eine weitere Konferenz sollte in der folgenden Woche einberufen werden.
2   Wir sollten den neuen Ausbildungsplan in der heutigen Sitzung vorstellen.
3   Wir sollten den Bericht heute vorlegen.
4   Sollte er eigentlich informiert werden?
5   Dieses Produkt sollte auf dem Markt nicht überleben.
6   Er sollte früh sterben.

7   Das sollte eine Überraschung für unseren neuen Kollegen werden.

8   Die Mitarbeiter sollten sich am Vorschlagswesen beteiligen.

2   You should do this/you ought to do this/you had better do this (i.e. *Sie sollten lieber*)

Make recommendations about future actions, choosing from the options suggested.

1   Sie sollten vielleicht mal einen Blick in Ihr Postfach werfen.

2   Wir müssten mehr für unsere Mitarbeiter tun.

3   Er sollte sich auf alle Fälle in der Sitzung sehen lassen.

4   Unsere Planung sollte sicher etwas effizienter gestaltet werden.

5   Ich meine, wir sollten Erkundigungen einziehen.

6   Sie sollten lieber dem Kunden Bescheid sagen.

7   Sie sollten lieber gleich beim Personalchef vorbeischauen.

3   Meeting expectations

Now attempt a different approach altogether – employing 'want to', 'would like to' and 'suggest that' to translate *'sollen'*. This is advisable when referring to other people's expectations or requests.

Examples

Warum sollte ich auf Sie warten?

Why did you want me to wait for you?

Why did you suggest that I (should) wait for you?

Soll ich Sie morgen treffen?

Would you like me to meet you tomorrow?

1   Soll ich das für Sie erledigen?

2   Warum sollte ich ihn interviewen?

3   Soll ich das für Sie wiederholen?

4   Soll ich etwas ausrichten?

5   Wo sollen wir warten?

6   Soll ich mir Ihre Telefonnummer aufschreiben?

2   *Dabei, damit, davon ...*

There is no 'standard' translation for ancillary prepositional constructions such as *dabei, damit, davon, dafür, darüber, darauf, darunter*, etc. which can stand for a full prepositional dative or accusative object. As the function of '*da* + preposition' is to create a connection to a previous statement, we must either translate the entire prepositional object (e.g. *bei der Verhandlung*) or search for an **Exercises** English phrase which serves the same purpose (e.g. 'in the course of ...', 'while doing this', 'in the process'). An active voice construction can also be a satisfactory solution. If *damit* modifies an adjective (e.g. *die damit verbundene Bedingung*) it is advisable to convert this adjective into a relative clause (see XII.3.3, Exercise 2, p. 173).

The above also applies to the much rarer genitive substitutes such as *deswegen* (objects and abstracts) and *deinetwegen* (persons) and their declined forms *meinet...*, *seinet...*, etc.

Example

It took a total of two months to complete the merger. In the course of the merger / during this process *(dabei, im Verlauf der Fusion)*, costs amounting to approximately 10 million dollars (UDS 10 million, $10 million) were incurred.

Alternative translation

Costs amounting to 10 million dollars were thereby incurred.

'Thereby' is considered to be dated; it is, however, quite common in contracts and legal documents. Please note also that it is rarely a translation of *dabei:* it more often translates *hiermit, somit, hierdurch*.

Example

Payroll costs increased last year, thereby causing our overall costs to rise: *Die Gehaltskosten sind letztes Jahr gestiegen, und somit auch die Gesamtkosten.*

Complete the following sentences.

1   *Öffnen Sie das Kopiergerät und entfernen Sie das Papier. Passen Sie auf, dass Sie sich dabei nicht verletzen.*
    Open the photocopier and remove the paper. Be careful not to injure yourself ___.

2   *Führungskräfte sollen die Unternehmensziele verfolgen und dabei die Förderung ihrer Mitarbeiter im Auge haben.*
    Senior executives are supposed to pursue their organisation's goals ___ staff development.

3   *Wegen der Produktionsverzögerung, beschlossen wir, die Teile per Luftfracht zu verschicken. Die damit verbundenen Mehrkosten wurden von unserer Firma übernommen.*
    Owing to the delay in production, we decided to airfreight the components. The additional costs ___ were covered by our company.

4   *Die Bremssysteme wurden in den letzten Jahren verbessert und damit auch insgesamt die Sicherheit der Fahrzeuge.*

In the last few years, braking systems have improved and ___ the overall safety of vehicles.

5 *Der Geschäftsführer lobte die Belegschaft wegen ihrer guten Leistung, die zu höherem Gewinn geführt hatte. Dabei/bei dieser Gelegenheit erwähnte er aber auch die höheren Rohölkosten.*

The Managing Director praised the staff for their good performance which had resulted in higher corporate profits. However, ___ he also mentioned the increase in crude oil prices.

6 *Wir akzeptieren Kreditkarten; denn dabei wird der Kunde begünstigt.*

We accept credit cards as ___ *(diese Zahlungsweise)* benefits the customer.

To make matters even more complicated, *dabei* can also be an independent adverb signifying *in Wirklichkeit*. In this case, it emphasizes the clash between a statement made and the actual state of affairs. 'Yet', 'but ... actually', 'but in fact', 'but the fact was', 'but in reality' serve a similar purpose in English.

Example

Er beklagte sich über die Arbeitsbelastung. Dabei hatte er weit weniger zu tun als die Kollegen. He complained about the workload. Yet he had far less to do than his colleagues.

VII Human Resources Management

VII Human Resources Management

VII.1 Text: Menschen führen ist wie Katzen dressieren

Der britische Management-Philosoph Charles Handy berichtet über einen Geschäftsführer, der sich damit brüstete, dass seine Erfolgs-gleichung „$^1/_2$ mal 2 mal 3 ist gleich Erfolg" sei. Der CEO erklärte, dass er mit einer halben Belegschaft zweimal soviel Waren produzieren könne bei einer Verdreifachung der Erträge. Nicht schlecht.

Aber, fragt Handy, „Was ist mit der anderen Hälfte?"

Warren Bennis befürchtet, dass angesichts der kolossalen Ein-kommenskluft in den Vereinigten Staaten, der weitreichenden Restrukturierung vieler Konzerne und der hohen Anzahl an Ar-beitslosen das nächste Jahrzehnt wohl „eine Zeit sozialer Unruhen wird, die in unserem Jahrhundert ihresgleichen suchen".

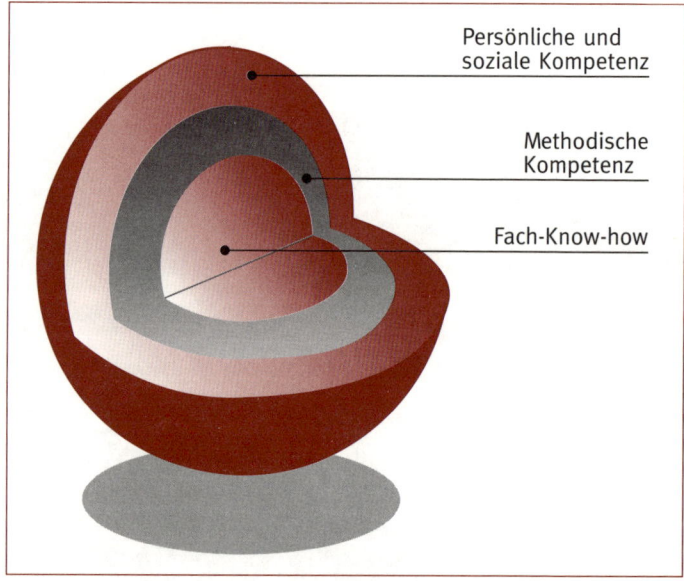

Persönliche und soziale Kompetenz

Methodische Kompetenz

Fach-Know-how

(adapted, CSC Ploenzke AG)

Für seine düstere Vision macht er die politischen und wirtschaftlichen Entscheidungsträger verantwortlich, denen er mangelnde Kenntnisse und Fähigkeiten in Bezug auf Menschenführung vorwirft.

Seit Mitte der 70er Jahre hat sich die Einkommenskluft zwischen den Superreichen und den Habenichtsen stark verbreitet. Damals „ver-fügte 1% der Bevölkerung über 18% des Privatvermögens", verglichen mit 40% heute. Das Verhältnis zwischen dem „durchschnittlichen

Gehalt von Führungskräften und der Entlohnung des Durchschnitts-
arbeiters wird auf 140:1 geschätzt". Aber während Geschäftsführer,
die in Folge von Fusionen oder sonstigen Umwälzungen ihre Position
verlieren, meist in Millionenhöhe abgefunden werden, „bekommen
Tausende von abgespeckten Mitarbeitern oft nur ein paar Monats-
gehälter als Trennungsentschädigung".

In den 50er Jahren glaubten etwa 70% der Amerikaner, dass ihre
Regierung „ehrlich um das Gemeinwohl besorgt sei", aber deren
Anzahl ist inzwischen auf 25% geschrumpft. Auch in Unternehmen ist
ein Großteil des früheren Vertrauens in die Führungskräfte verloren
gegangen, weil die Arbeitnehmer sich machtlos und demoralisiert
fühlen anstelle „sich mit der Art von kreativer Problemlösung zu
befassen, die heutige Unternehmen brauchen". Immer mehr Firmen
setzen deshalb auf echte Beteiligung ihrer Mitarbeiter an unternehmerischen Entscheidungsprozessen, eine Entwicklung, die unter
dem Stichwort „Empowerment" im vergangenen Jahrzehnt häufig in
der Fachliteratur diskutiert wurde.

Tatsache aber ist, dass sich „Empowerment" derzeit auf einem
Kollisionskurs mit einem weiteren Modebegriff des Management, und
zwar dem des „Business Process Reengineering" (BPR) befindet. BPR
steht für radikale, kostenbeeinflusste Umstrukturierungsmaßnahmen,
wie z.B. die Fremdbeschaffung von Teilen, die Ausgründung von Nicht-
Kernbereichen und die Verschlankung der Mitarbeiter, und führt somit
fast unvermeidlich zum Verlust von Arbeitsplätzen.

„Kann es Empowerment ohne Vertrauen geben?" fragt Bennis.
Seiner Ansicht nach muss der private Sektor sich auf die
Gratwanderung zwischen Profitorientierung und Schaffung
einer Vertrauenskultur begeben. Die Personalchefs stehen bei
diesem Unterfangen an der vordersten Front. Sie müssen wieder
lernen, die Menschen in ihrem Unternehmen zu schätzen, damit sie
deren innovatives Potential anzapfen können.

Zusammenfassend stellt Warren fest: Menschenführung ist eine
Begabung, die der Fähigkeit, Katzen zu dressieren, in nichts
nachsteht. Zweifelsohne ist es für ein Unternehmen keine geringe
Aufgabe, seine betrieblichen Prozesse komplett umzustrukturieren
und gleichzeitig seine Mitarbeiter aktiv in Management-Ent-
scheidungen zu integrieren. Wo es jedoch gelingt, bleibt der
finanzielle Erfolg nicht aus.

(M. Seidenspinner, On "Managing People is like Herding Cats, W.
Bennis on Leadership", Kogan Page, London, 1998)

Managing people is like herding cats

British management philosopher Charles Handy wrote about a **CEO**[1] who boasted that his equation for success was **"half times two times three equals success**[2]**"**. The CEO explained that with half the workforce he could produce twice as many goods with three times the **revenues**[3]. Not bad. But, Handy asks, 'What about the other half?"

Warren Bennis fears that, **in view of the colossal income gap**[4] in the United States, the **extensive**[5] restructuring of many major corporations, and the high number of unemployed, the next decade will probably be "a period of **social unrest unequalled in this century**[6]**"**.

He **blames** his **bleak vision**[7] on the political and economic **decision makers**[8]**, whom he accuses of lacking the knowledge and skills required for**[9] the management of people.

The disparity between the **haves and the have-nots**[10] has widened tremendously. In the mid-70s, "one percent of the population **controlled**[11] eighteen percent of **private wealth**[12]" compared to 40 percent today, and the **estimated ratio**[13] between the "average salary of CEOs and the pay of workers is now 140 to 1".

But whereas top managers who have lost their **office**[14] due to **mergers**[15] or other corporate upheavals usually receive **a golden handshake**[16], "the **downsized**[17] thousands get a few months' **severance pay**[18]**."**

In the '50s, about 70 percent of Americans believed that their government was **genuinely concerned about the common good**[19], but their number has **meanwhile dwindled to a mere 25 per cent**[20]. In the corporations, too, **a great deal of the trust formerly placed in the executives**[21] has been lost as workers feel powerless and demoralized **instead of "engaging in**[22] the kind of creative problem solving that **contemporary**[23] business requires."

An increasing number of corporations therefore **rely on**[24] the participation of their staff in corporate decision processes, a development which has, in the past ten years, frequently been discussed in the specialist literature **under the label of 'employee empowerment'**[25].

It is, however, a fact that 'empowerment' currently finds itself on a collision course with another management **buzzword**[26]**, namely that of, 'business process reengineering' (BPR)**[27]. BPR stands for radical, **cost-driven**[29] restructuring measures such as the **outsourcing**[29] of components, the **hiving off of non-core areas**[30] and the downsizing of the workforce, and thereby almost inevitably results in **job losses**[31].

"Can there be empowerment **in the absence of**[32] trust?", asks Bennis. In his view, the private sector must **undertake to walk the tightrope**[33] between profit orientation and the generation of a **high trust culture**[34]. The Human Resource Managers will find themselves **at the forefront**[35] of this **venture**[36]. They will have to learn once more to value the people in their enterprise, in order to tap their innovative potential.

Summing it up, Warren maintains that managing people is **a skill on a par with the ability to herd cats**[37]. Without any doubt it is **no mean task**[38] for a corporation to completely restructure its business operations while simultaneously integrating its staff in the managerial decision taking. But wherever this is achieved, **it is bound to result in financial success**[39].

2.1 Notes on the translation

● ● ● ● ● ● ● ●

[1] *Geschäftsführer:* CEO

For detailed explanations see V.2.1, note [6], p. 68.

[2] *¹/₂ mal 2 mal 3 ist gleich Erfolg:* half times two times three equals success

The fast version of mathematical equations such as '2 x 3 equals 6' is 'two threes are six'.

[3] *Erträge:* revenues; (sales) takings

← Please note

> According to German 'accounting principles' *(Grundsätze der Rechnungslegung)* a pragmatic – and dogmatic – distinction is made between *Einnahmen* and *Erträge*, but Anglo-American usage, which is based on the 'cash-flow statement' *(also: 'statement of cash receipts and disbursements': Kapitalflussrechnung)*, is by no means as clear-cut.
>
> Very much to the dismay of some students of Business Administration, who are taught never to confuse *'Einnahmen'* with *'Erträge'*, the English terms 'income' and 'revenues' do exactly that.
>
> • *Einnahmen:* gross income; total revenues; also: takings; receipts.
> *Einnahmen* are the 'gross income' of an individual, a group or a business over a period of time which increases the private wealth of a person or group as well as the 'financial assets' *(Geldvermögen)* of a company. It derives mainly from the sales of products or services but also from other 'cash-less income' *(unbare Einnahmen)* or 'incidental receipts'

(gelegentliche Einnahmen) such as the 'proceeds' *(Verkaufserlöse)* accruing from financial and property transactions.

- *Erträge:* revenues; income
  Erträge are periodical income items which include 'turnover' or 'sales revenues' *(Umsatzerlöse)* from continuing operations and acquisitions as well as 'other operating income' *(sonstige betriebliche Erträge)*, e.g. from rentals, leasing *(Vermietung, Verpachtung)*, licences, patents, and income derived from 'shares' *(Erträge aus Beteiligungen)* and investments *(Erträge aus Finanzanlagen)*.
  In a company's annual 'income statement' or 'profit and loss account' ('P&L a/c'; *Gewinn- und Verlustrechnung, G+V)* this type of income or 'revenues' *(Erträge)* is juxtaposed with 'expenses' *(Aufwendungen)*. Cf. XII.2.1.note [26], p. 167.

4 *angesichts der kollosalen Einkommenskluft:* in view of the colossal income gap; faced with the gigantic income disparity/ discrepancy
A further possible translation would be 'income divide' *(Einkommensgefälle)* which is formed like 'North-South divide' *(Nord-Süd-Gefälle)*. This expression emphasises the disparity in wealth between the northern and the southern hemispheres.

5 *weitreichend:* extensive; far-reaching
Restructuring can also be characterised as 'intensive', i.e. 'profound' *(tiefgründig)*, 'thorough' *(gründlich)* or 'comprehensive' *(umfassend)*.

6 *eine Zeit sozialer Unruhen, die in unserem Jahrhundert ihresgleichen suchen:* a period of social unrest unequalled in our century; a period of social unrest unparallelled/unrivalled in our century
Further possible translation of *ihresgleichen suchen* is 'which will put other periods of unrest in the shade'; 'which will dwarf other periods of unrest'.

Please note →

> Note that 'unrest' has no plural form; also note the US spellings of 'unequaled', 'unrivaled', 'unparalleled'.

7 *für seine düstere Vision macht er ... verantwortlich:* he blames his bleak vision on; he blames his sombre vision on
For the significance of 'vision' in corporate strategy see VI.2.1, note [15], p. 82.

[8] *Entscheidungsträger:* decision makers; decision takers

[9] *denen er mangelnde Kenntnisse und Fähigkeiten in Bezug auf …*
vorwirft: whom he accuses of lacking the knowledge and skills
required for; whom he accuses of lacking the knowledge and skills
when it comes to/with regard to/regarding/as far as … is concerned

> 'Knowledge' is 'the result of informed learning' whereas 'skills'
> are specific abilities which have to be acquired by continuous
> practice.
> 'Knowledge', like *Wissen,* has no plural form.

← Please note

[10] *die Superreichen und die Habenichtse:* the 'haves' and the 'have-
nots'; the very rich and the very poor
The British press often labels the 'super rich' as 'fat cats'.

[11] *verfügte über:* controlled
The verb 'to control' is usually rendered as *steuern,* e.g. in remote-
controlled: *ferngesteuert.* See also II.2.1, note [13], p. 29.

[12] *Privatvermögen:* private wealth; private assets

[13] *das Verhältnis wird auf … geschätzt:* the estimated ratio … is; the
ratio is … estimated to be

[14] *die ihre Position verloren haben:* who have lost their office; who
have lost their position

[15] *Fusionen:* mergers; see XII.2.1, note [4], p. 163.

[16] *Abfindung:* a golden handshake; a golden parachute; redundancy
pay; termination pay

> The colloquial idiom 'to be given a golden handshake' is
> possibly the best translation in view of the sheer volume of the
> financial compensation paid to CEOs who lose their office. A
> similar idea is expressed in the German saying: *Er lässt sich den*
> *Abschied versilbern.* 'To be offered a golden parachute' implies
> a slight note sarcasm: it is mostly used for industrial leaders
> who were made (or would have been made) redundant because
> of their lack of valuable contribution.

← Please note

[17] *abgespeckt:* downsized

> 'Downsizing' (in colloquial US usage 'rightsizing') is the
> reduction in size of parts of an organisation in order to save
> costs and/or to increase productivity. The expected outcome is
> that of a 'leaner' *(schlanker)* organisation which is more
> profitable and more efficient.

← Please note

‘Downsizing measures’ mostly affect the payroll staff, but also operational and service areas (e.g. non-core units, component production, warehousing facilities).

See also ‘delayering’ in V.2.1, note [15], p. 70 and ‘outsourcing’ in note [29], p. 99.

[18] *Trennungsentschädigung:* severance pay. See also note [16] above.

[19] *dass sie ehrlich um das Gemeinwohl besorgt sei:* that it was genuinely concerned about the common good; that it was truly / honestly concerned about the common good

In British English the plural verb form ‘the government were honestly concerned about’ is also possible.

[20] *ist inzwischen auf nur 25% geschrumpft:* has meanwhile dwindled to a mere 25 per cent (also: percent); has dwindled to only 25 per cent in the meantime; has since then dwindled to a mere 25 per cent

[21] *ein Großteil des früheren Vertrauens in die Führungskräfte:* a great deal of the trust formerly placed in the executives; a fair amount of the trust formerly placed in the management

For *‘Führungskräfte’* see V.2.1, note [6], p. 67.

[22] *anstelle sich mit … zu befassen mit:* instead of engaging in; instead of committing themselves to; instead of focussing on

[23] *zeitgemäße Unternehmen:* contemporary business

‘Contemporary’, like the German *zeitgemäß*, implies ‘confirming to modern or current ideas’.

[24] *auf etwas setzen:* to rely on; to count on

[25] *unter dem Stichwort ‘employee empowerment’:* under the label of ‘employee empowerment’

‘Empowerment’ is a neologism in German; it is not translated.

Please note →

In Human Resource Management, ‘empowerment’ signifies the delegation of responsibility and managerial power (especially with a view to decision-making) to the employees at the ‘front line’ (e.g. the ‘shop floor’).

This concept is based on the belief that a higher level of responsibility and authority (‘job enrichment’: *vertikale Aufgabenerweiterung*) and a wider range of professional tasks (‘job enlargement’: *Ausweitung des Aufgabenfeldes*) will lead to personal satisfaction and hence a higher level of co-operation and commitment. On the other hand, ‘empowerment’ also increases the level of 'staff accountability' *(Verantwort-lichkeit der Mitarbeiter)* and the delayering of corporate hierarchies (see V.2.1, note [15], p. 70).

[26] *Modebegriff des Management:* management buzzword; business buzzword; fashionable management term

> A 'buzzword' is an expression that suddenly becomes a vogue, often in connection with a specific type of jargon. In business theory, 'buzzwords' often accompany 'management fads' (i.e. intense, short-lived crazes or fashions).

← Please note

[27] *und zwar dem des "Business Process Reengineering":* namely that of Business Process Reengineering

> 'BPR' stands for a major 'reorganisation and restructuring of business processes': *Um- und Neustrukturierung der Betriebs-prozesse.* It is mostly implemented in production, logistics and warehousing, e.g. by introducing task-focussed work cells, concurrent production and JIT deliveries. 'BPR' has frequently been criticized for its focus on processes while neglecting the human factor which constitutes a vital element of the TQM philosophy (see IX.2.1, note [3], p. 123).

← Please note

[28] *kostenbeeinflusste:* cost-driven; also: cost-cutting *(kosten-senkend)*

[29] *Fremdbeschaffung:* outsourcing

> 'Outsourcing' is the purchasing of semi-finished or finished products, components or services from subcontractors or suppliers rather than providing these products or services internally at a higher cost level.

← Please note

[30] *Ausgründung von Nicht-Kernbereichen:* the hiving off of non-core areas
'to hive off' means 'to split off' or 'sell' of parts of a company.
For 'non-core areas' see V.2.1, note [21], p. 72.

[31] *Verlust an Arbeitsplätzen:* job losses

> *Arbeitsplatz* is a polysemous noun. Literally it means 'place of work', but it also acts as a metonym for 'job'. In English, these two lexical items form separate semantic entitities and the translator has to decide which one is appropriate. In this case, it is the 'job' which is lost not the 'place of work'.

← Please note

● ● ● ● ● ● ● ●

For further usage examples see *Arbeitsplatz* III.2.1, note [9], p. 42 and *Büroplatz* III.2.1, note [20], p. 46. See also VII.3.2.

[32] *ohne:* in the absence of; without

[33] *eine Gratwanderung auf sich nehmen:* undertake to walk the tightrope; accept the challenge to walk the tight-rope

[34] *Vertrauenskultur:* high trust culture

Please note →

> In cultural anthropology, 'high trust cultures' are contrasted with 'low trust cultures'. Especially in Western Europe businesses are said to be hampered by low trust, which entails a whole series of other negative types of behaviour such as the incapability of admitting to mistakes.

[35] *an der vordersten Front:* at the forefront; at the frontline

[36] *Unterfangen:* venture; see also III.2.1, note [14], p. 44.

[37] *ein Kunststück, das der Katzendressur in nichts nachsteht:* a skill on a par with the ability to herd cats; a skill only rivalled by the ability to herd cats

Please note →

> The 'cat herding' metaphor is fairly popular in HRM publications. As there is no similar idiom in German, *Katzen dressieren* seems the most likely translation: it is a well-known fact that cats have defeated all attempts to make them perform on request.

[38] *keine geringe (gerinzuschätzende) Aufgabe:* no mean task

[39] *bleibt der finanzielle Erfolg nicht aus:* it is bound to result in financial succes; financial success is sure to follow / to ensue

VII. 3 Exercises

3.1. Terminology: managing change

Please fill the gaps using the terms and phrases provided in the notes.

1 An overwhelming number of managers see ___ *(weitgehende)* organisational changes such as the ___ *(Verschlankung)* of staff numbers and the ___ *(Neuorganisation)* of critical business processes exclusively from a ___ *(kostensparendem)* point of view, and this inevitably seems to result in severe ___ *(Arbeitsplatzverluste)*.

2 ___ *(Beteiligung der Mitarbeiter an Entscheidungsprozessen)* involves the delegation of ___ *(Verantwortung)* and power to the ___ *(vorderste Front)* where strategies are put to the test.

3 This necessarily entails a ___ *(Verflachung)* of the management hierarchy which ___ *(sich auswirkt)* in particular the middle management level.

4 A further downside of empowerment is that employees become directly ___ *(verantwortlich)* for deficient products and processes.

5 However, improved ___ ___ *(Arbeitszufriedenheit)*, job ___ *(vertikale Aufgabenerweiterung)* and job ___ *(Ausweitung des Arbeitsfeldes)* have proved to have a positive impact on ___ *(Produktivität)*.

6 When top executives lose their office, they usually receive ___ ___ *(Trennungsentschädigung)* which is also known as a ___ ___ *(versilberter Abschied)*.

7 Western European companies are notorious for their *(Atmosphäre des Misstrauens)* ___ ___ which discourages staff ___ *(Engagement)* and impedes even well-functioning teams.

8 It is therefore the most important task of a corporate leader to create a ___ ___ ___ *(Vertrauensklima)* in his or her organisation.

9 Warren forecasts social unrest in the US which will ___ the protests of the sixties and early seventies ___ *(in den Schatten stellen)*.

10 ___ *(Fremdbeschaffung)*, the more cost-effective procurement of ___ *(Teile)* from affiliated or allied partners, has to be based on a well-founded "make or buy" decision.

3.2 Tricky translations: places and spaces

Platz seems an innocuous enough noun to translate but as the following examples will show, this is a misconception.

> court • desk • extra space • football pitch • jobs • office space • parking lot • place • seat • Square • standing capacity • way

Test your translation skills with these sentences. Include the suggestions made in the grey box.

1 Es steht mir nicht zu, Ihr Verhalten zu beurteilen.
2 Der Bus hat 20 Sitzplätze und 35 Stehplätze.
3 Richard Branson soll die meisten Geschäfte auf dem Tennisplatz abschließen.
4 Sonntags findest du Carl auf dem hiesigen Fußballplatz.
5 Wir haben einen tollen Blick auf den „Schlossplatz".
6 Bitte nehmen Sie doch Platz.
7 Wir müssen für die neue Ware zusätzlichen Platz schaffen.
8 BPR hat einige Unternehmen wettbewerbsfähiger gemacht aber auch viele Arbeitsplätze gekostet.
9 Bitte stellen Sie Ihren Wagen auf dem neuen Parkplatz ab.

10 Leider ist Mr. Brown nicht an seinem Platz.

11 John and Laura teilen sich zur Zeit ihren Büroplatz.

12 Platz da!

3.3 Additional practice: opposites

Translate the following adjectives with the help of a dictionary. Note that the English usage is as erratic as the German one and that there may be more than one option.

1 bedeutende/unbedeutende Ereignisse

2 glaubwürdige/unglaubwürdige Geschichte

3 gut lesbarer/unleserlicher Text

4 kritikwürdige/untadelige Manieren

5 lösbares/unlösbares Problem

6 mangelhafte/tadellose Qualität

7 nachvollziehbar/nicht nachvollziehbar

8 passendes/unpassendes Beispiel

9 verantwortungsvolle/unverantwortliche Entscheidung

10 vergleichbare/nicht vergleichbare Ergebnisse

11 vermeidbares/unvermeidbares Risiko

12 verständliche/unverständliche Aussage

13 verzeihlicher/unverzeihlicher Irrtum

14 verzichtbar/unverzichtbare Bedingung

15 vorstellbare/unvorstellbare Folgen

16 widerrufliches/unwiderrufliches Akkreditiv

17 zugängliche/unzugängliche Daten

Work out the difference between the following adjectives.

18 nicht vergleichbar – unvergleichliche Leistung

19 unglaubwürdige – unglaubliche Geschichte

20 unleserlicher – nicht lesbarer Text

21 nicht wiedererkennbare – unverkennbare Bilder

VIII Employee Participation

VIII Employee Participation

VIII.1 Text: Warum Mitarbeiter-beteiligung?

Mitarbeiterbeteiligung hat drei Komponenten: die Erfolgs-, die Kapital- und die immaterielle Beteiligung.

Unter Erfolgsbeteiligung versteht man Beteiligungsformen, bei denen die Mitarbeiter zusätzlich zu Grundlohn und -gehalt eine erfolgsabhängige Zuwendung erhalten.

Bei der Kapitalbeteiligung stellt der Mitarbeiter dem Unternehmen Kapital zur Verfügung – als Fremdkapital, als Eigenkapital oder in einer Mischform; die Kapitalentlohnung orientiert sich in der Regel wiederum am Erfolg des Unternehmens.

Immaterielle Beteiligung bedeutet die engere Einbindung der Mitarbeiter in die Unternehmensprozesse durch verstärkte Kommunikation und Information.

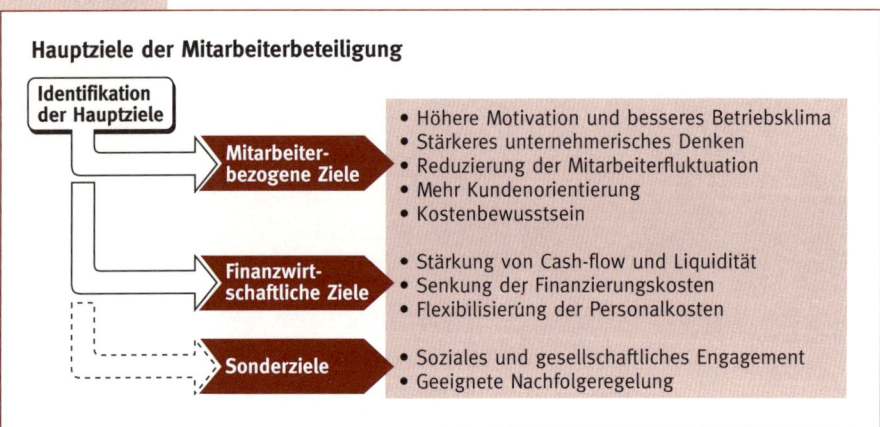

Hauptziele der Mitarbeiterbeteiligung

Identifikation der Hauptziele

Mitarbeiter-bezogene Ziele
- Höhere Motivation und besseres Betriebsklima
- Stärkeres unternehmerisches Denken
- Reduzierung der Mitarbeiterfluktuation
- Mehr Kundenorientierung
- Kostenbewusstsein

Finanzwirt-schaftliche Ziele
- Stärkung von Cash-flow und Liquidität
- Senkung der Finanzierungskosten
- Flexibilisierung der Personalkosten

Sonderziele
- Soziales und gesellschaftliches Engagement
- Geeignete Nachfolgeregelung

In erfolgreichen Mitarbeiterbeteiligungsmodellen werden diese drei Komponenten häufig verknüpft; dabei dient die Erfolgsbeteiligung ganz oder teilweise dazu, die Mittel für die Kapitalbeteiligung aufzubringen.

Das Besondere der Mitarbeiterbeteiligung: Richtig konzipiert, schafft sie einen „Mehrwert", von dem beide Seiten, Arbeitnehmer und Unternehmen, profitieren. Die Mitarbeiter sind am Unternehmenserfolg beteiligt, sie erzielen Kapitaleinkommen und können so ihren Wohlstand sichern. Die damit verbundene hohe Motivation wiederum stärkt das Unternehmen insgesamt, was zu größeren Gewinnen auch für die Eigentümer führt.

(McKinsey & Company, Inc.)

What are the reasons behind employee participation schemes?

Employee participation[1] comprises three elements: **profit and gain sharing**[2], **employee capital sharing**[3] and **non-material**[4] forms of participation. **The terms** profit and gain sharing **generally mean**[5] forms of participation in which the employees **are allocated**[6] a **profit-related or performance-related**[7] **bonus**[8] in addition to their **basic wage or salary**[9]. Capital sharing means that the employees provide the company with capital – either as **loan capital**[10] or as **equity capital**[11], or as a mixture of the two. As a rule, **the income derived from this capital**[12] **is** also **related to**[13] the performance of the company.

Non-material participation means **the closer involvement**[14] of the employees in the company's strategic processes **by means of**[15] increased communication and information. Successful **employee participation plans**[16] often **link these three components**[17]; **in such cases**[18], **profit-sharing schemes may serve, or partially serve**[19], **to provide the employees with the financial resources**[20] needed for capital investment and equity ownership.

The special characteristic of[21] employee participation schemes is that, **if they are properly designed**[22], they create "added value", from which both parties, **employees**[23] and **employers**[24], **benefit**[25]. The employees participate in the success of the company; they **gain an investment income**[26] and can thus **secure**[27] their own **prosperity**[28]. In turn, **the stronger motivation that goes along with this**[29] strengthens the company as a whole, **leading to**[30] higher profits for the owners as well.

VIII.2.1 Sample translation

2.1 Notes on the Translation

[1]   *Mitarbeiterbeteiligung:* employee participation; employee participation schemes/plans; co-partnerships; co-participation plans

← Please note

> The compound 'employee participation' conveys, above all, the idea of a partnership between the employer and the employee, an idea which is also suggested by 'co-partnership' *(Mitbeteiligung)* or 'co-partnership system' and 'co-partnership scheme'.
>
> Apart from the non-material forms of participation, there are two essential types of employee participation, namely
> - *Erfolgsbeteiligung/Gewinnbeteiligung:* 'profit and gain sharing plans' which peg contingent pay cheques to corporate performance (see note [2] below).

- *Kapitalbeteiligung:* various 'capital (investment) and equity sharing schemes' between the employees and their employers (see note [3] below).

Especially within the German tradition, 'employee participation' has a further aspect, namely enabling employees to take part in the management and control of the company. In this case, it may be translated as *Arbeitnehmerbeteiligung, betriebliche Mitbestimmung.* Further English terms for this reading of 'employee participation' are: 'codetermination', 'worker participation', 'shop floor participation', 'worker say'.

[2] *Erfolgsbeteiligung:* profit and gain sharing; a share in the company's profits; performance-related contingent pay

Please note →

- 'Profit sharing': *Gewinnbeteiligung, finanzielle Beteiligung am Unternehmensgewinn.* These schemes comprise any arrangement whereby bonuses and other forms of additional pay are linked to corporate performance which can be measured or rated (see note [7] below).
- 'Gain sharing' may be rendered as *Beteiligung am Produktivitätszuwachs*, but this narrows down the scope of the term. 'Gain sharing plans' measure and reward collective contributions of work teams whose contingent pay is based on the varying results achieved by them. 'Gain sharing schemes' are mostly practised in production, but they could also be relevant in other areas such as customer services. Gain sharing is intended to provide group incentives which may be linked to other variables than profitability.

[3] *Kapitalbeteiligung:* employee capital sharing; employee capital participation; capital sharing between employers and employees; employee equity ownership and capital investment schemes

Please note →

In the model described here, 'employee capital sharing' comprises two distinct components:
- 'Equity ownership' represents a form of capital sharing in which employees are offered the chance to own some of their company's 'equity capital' (see note [11] below) e.g. by buying its shares. These programmes are also referred to as 'employee share ownership', 'employee shareholding', 'employee stock ownership'.

Some companies operate 'employee share purchase plans'/ 'employee stock purchase plans': *Programme für den Erwerb von Belegschaftsaktien.*
As well as motivating employees to perform better, 'employee stock ownership plans' or 'ESOPs' are employed in the US as 'company pension plans' *(Betriebsrentenpläne).* The stock is 'held in trust' *(unter treuhänderischer Verwaltung)* for the employees as the basis for their 'retirement incomes' *(Altersversorgung).*

- 'Capital investment' is provided by the workers who – acting as 'creditors' *(Gläubiger)* – grant their company a loan which may be identical with the bonus they have received. This does not give the employees any rights to ownership.

4 *immateriell:* non-material; intangible

- 'Immaterial' is a false friend. It signifies 'irrelevant', 'unimportant', 'inconsequential'.
  Example
  The price is immaterial: *Der Preis spielt keine Rolle.*
- 'Intangible' literally means 'cannot be touched' whereas 'tangible' implies a physical existence.

← Please note

In 'balance sheet accounting' *(Bilanzierung)* corporate assets are divided into 'fixed assets' *(Anlagevermögen)* and 'current assets' *(Umlaufvermögen).*

- 'Fixed assets' include:
  'intangible assets' *(immaterielle Vermögensgegenstände),* which may be 'concessions' *(Konzessionen),* 'goodwill' *(der Geschäfts- oder Firmenwert)* and 'payments on account' *(geleistete Anzahlungen)*
  'tangible assets', which are land, buildings and the equipment used to create corporate wealth
  'financial assets', *(Finanzanlagen)* such as long term investments.
- 'Current assets' are 'stocks' *(Vorräte)* of raw materials, 'work in progress' *(unfertige Erzeugnisse)* and 'finished goods' *(fertige Erzeugnisse),* 'trade debtors' (see X.2.1, note [18], p. 139), 'securities' *(Wertpapiere),* 'cash in hand' *(Kassenbestand)* and 'bank balances' *(Bankguthaben).*

●●●●●●●●   5   *unter … versteht man:* the terms … generally mean; the terms can be defined as; the terms may be defined as

6   *erhalten:* are allocated; are granted; are awarded; are paid
For additional practice see 3.2., Exercise 1: Obtain and receive, p. 114.

7   *erfolgsabhängig:* profit-related or performance-related

Please note →

> *Erfolgsabhängig* may be synonymous with *gewinnabhängig* ('profit-related'), but the significance of *Erfolg* is defined by each organisation individually. Most of them link their entrepreneurial 'success' to the difference between the expenditure and the revenue-related results of their corporate activities which are stated in the proverbial 'bottom line' *(Saldo: Nettogewinn oder Nettoverlust, der 'unterm Strich' herauskommt)* of their annual income statements.
> This 'bottom line' is regarded as an indicator of the overall corporate performance. In addition, 'performance' can be measured by the increase in the company's share price over a set period, or the performance of the share price compared with other stocks in a specified index.
> In HRM, 'performance' denotes the achievements of an individual employee. Pay cheques that mirror employee contributions are therefore called 'performance-related pay' or 'merit pay': *leistungsgerechte/leistungsorientierte Entlohnung.*

8   *Zuwendung:* bonus; bonus payment; contingent pay

> Whereas 'payment' denotes either a 'sum of money paid' or the 'act of paying' itself, a 'bonus' *(Prämie, Zulage)* is a 'contingent payment', which may represent a reward.

Certain semantic aspects of *Zuwendung* are contained in the verbs that collocate with translantions of it, e.g. 'to be allocated', 'to be granted'. Other translations of *Zuwendung*, which might be appropriate in different contexts, are:
(financial) contribution: *Beitrag*
donation: *Spende*
legacy/bequest: *Nachlass, vererbte Zuwendung*
endowments: *Stiftungsgelder*
subsidy: *Subvention*
handout (informal): *Zuwendung, Unterstützung*

allowance: *Freibetrag, Pauschale, Beihilfe, Taschengeld, Unterhalt*

grant: *Subvention, Stipendium*

benefit: *Zuschuss, Beihilfe*

gratuity: *Gratifikation, Geldgeschenk, Trinkgeld*

perk (informal), fringe benefit: *gehaltsunabhängige Zusatzleistung, Zusatzvergütung, Vergünstigung*

ex gratia payment: *freiwillige Zuwendung*

9 *Grundlohn und -gehalt:* basic wage or salary; basic pay; basic compensation; basic remuneration; basic pay check (US)

← Please note

> Production workers may be paid 'an hourly or weekly wage' *(Stunden- oder Wochenlohn)* or receive a 'monthly pay cheque' (Monatslohn). They may also be paid 'piece rate' *(Stücklohn, Akkord)*. Office workers usually receive a 'monthly salary' *(monatliches Gehalt)*.
>
> The generic terms for money received in exchange for work are 'pay' *(Bezahlung, Entlohnung)*, 'compensation' (US) and 'remuneration' *(Vergütung)*.

Some common collocations in this context are

pay negotiations: *Lohn-, Gehaltsverhandlungen; Tarifverhandlungen* (when these negotiations are conducted by the trades unions they are known as 'collective bargaining')

pay award/pay rise; pay hike (US): *Lohn-, Gehaltserhöhung*

equal pay: *gleiche Entlohnung, gleicher Lohn*

take-home pay: *Nettoverdienst, tatsächliches Gehalt*

pay policy; compensation policy (US): *Lohn- und Gehaltspolitik*

executive pay: *Gehälter für Führungskräfte/leitende Angestellte*

minimum wage: *Mindestlohn*

draw a salary: *ein Gehalt beziehen*

> Note that, in British English, compensation usually means 'damages', i.e. 'payment to make up for damage or a loss': *Schadenersatz* or *Schmerzensgeld*.

10 *Fremdkapital:* loan capital; debt capital; borrowed capital
This is capital borrowed from, e.g., a bank, or, in the above participation model, from the employees (see note [3], item 2).

11 *Eigenkapital:* equity capital; equity; stockholders' equity

In public limited companies the 'equity capital' consists of 'reserves' *(Rücklagen)* and the share capital *(Stammkapital)* which has been invested by the proprietors or the shareholders of a company and is therefore owned by them. See also: note ³, item 1.

The ratio between a company's 'ordinary share capital' and its 'loan capital' is referred to as 'gearing' *(Verschuldungsgrad)*. A company with a high proportion of loaned capital is said to have a 'high gearing' or to be 'high geared' *(mit hohem Fremdkapitalanteil)*.

12 *Kapitalentlohnung:* the income derived from this capital; any earnings from this capital investment; the capital yield

> Note that *'Kapitalentlohnung'* here corresponds to *Kapital-ertrag.*

13 *orientiert sich:* is related to; is linked to; is tied to
Further examples of how to translate *sich orientieren*
Der Preis orientiert sich am Gewicht: The price depends on the weight.
Der Preis orientiert sich an der Marktnachfrage: The price depends on/is determined by/is linked to market demand.
Sich in einer fremden Stadt zu orientieren (zurechtzufinden) ist nicht immer leicht. It's not always easy to find one's way around/ to get one's bearings in a strange town.
For additional practice on reflexive verbs see 3.3 below, p. 116.

14 *die engere Einbindung:* the closer involvement; involving (the employees) more closely

15 *durch:* by means of; through

16 *(Mitarbeiterbeteiligungs-) Modelle:* plans; schemes; programmes; models

On the whole, 'model' tends to denote a 'design or type of product', rather than a 'plan' or 'scheme'.
Examples
We will be demonstrating this year's model at the Hanover Fair: *Wir werden unser diesjähriges Modell auf der Hannover Messe vorführen.*
a prototype model: *ein Prototyp*
the standard model: *die Standardausführung, das Standard-modell*

> 'Model' can also be a theoretical construct.
> Like the perfect competition model, the monopoly model is rarely found in practice.

[17] *in erfolgreichen Mitarbeitermodellen werden diese drei Komponenten oft verknüpft:* successful employee participation plans often link these three components; in successful employee participation plans, these three components are often linked

> If an active voice construction is possible, as in the above case, native speakers are more likely to employ it.
> Examples
> *In den Zeitungen wurde viel über die Fusion berichtet.* The press/the newspapers reported extensively on the merger.
> *Den Mitarbeitern wurde von der Firma die Möglichkeit geboten, Belegschaftsaktien zu kaufen:* The company offered employees the opportunity to buy shares in it.

[18] *dabei:* in such cases; when this is the case
Dabei stands for a whole phrase *(bei einer solchen Verknüpfung).* For a detailed description of the grammatical complexity of *'dabei'* and similar constructions see VI.3.3, Exercise 2, p. 88.

[19] *dient die Erfolgsbeteiligung ganz oder teilweise dazu:* profit-sharing schemes may serve, or partially serve to; the aim/purpose, or part of the aim/purpose of profit-sharing schemes may be to

[20] *die Mittel für ... aufzubringen:* to provide the employees with the financial resources needed for

> This is an example of how a translator may wish to make explicit something (i.e. 'the employees') which is implicit in the original text.

In general, the collocation *die Mittel aufbringen* may be translated as 'to raise the (financial) resources/funds/finance/money/capital'.
Example
We managed to raise sufficient funds to avoid insolvency. *Wir konnten die Mittel aufbringen, um Zahlungsunfähigkeit zu umgehen.*

[21] *das Besondere an:* the special characteristic of; the special/distinctive thing about; the special/distinctive feature of; what is special/distinctive/particularly important about ...

Employee Participation 111

Adjectives can be turned into nouns in German. Here are some further examples together with possible translations.

das Interessante an diesem Plan: the interesting thing about this plan; what is interesting about this plan

das Ungewöhnliche an diesem Layout: the unusual feature of/ the unusual thing about this layout; what is unusual about this layout

das Schwierigste an meiner Arbeit: the most difficult part of my job

²² *richtig konzipiert, ...:* if they are properly designed; if they are designed properly; if they are worked out in the right way; if they are planned correctly/sensibly

For additional practice on adjectives vs. adverbs see I.3.3 Exercise 1, p. 20.

Further translations of *konzipiert* are 'conceived' and 'thought out'. The related noun, *Konzept*, may be rendered as 'plan', 'draft', 'design' or 'idea'.

• Examples
Schicken Sie mir bitte das Konzept für die Präsentation per E-Mail. Please e-mail me the draft presentation.
Wir haben ein gutes Konzept für die Präsentation; jetzt müssen wir es auch zu Papier bringen. We have a good idea for the presentation; now we have to put it down on paper.

• 'To conceive of' means 'to imagine' or 'to believe'.
Example
You cannot conceive of the difficulty we had in designing this programme. *Sie können sich die Schwierigkeiten nicht vorstellen, die wir beim Konzipieren dieses Programms hatten.*

Related nouns are 'idea' or 'concept'.
Example
The idea/concept of employee profit sharing has existed for a long time in many countries. *Die Idee, die Mitarbeiter am Unternehmensgewinn zu beteiligen, besteht seit langem in vielen Ländern.*

²³ *Arbeitnehmer:* employees; the workforce; staff
For detailed explanations see I.2.1, note ¹¹, p. 13.

²⁴ *Unternehmen:* here: the employer(s) (as this pairs nicely with 'employees')

112

[25] *profitieren:* benefit, profit, gain
For the difference between 'profit' and 'gain' see IV.2.1, note [6], p. 56.

[26] *Kapitaleinkommen erzielen:* gain an investment income; obtain a capital income
'Unearned income' *(Einkommen aus Vermögen)* can also translate *Kapitaleinkommen*, but not usually in collocation with 'gain' and 'receive'.

Example
Since the sale of the property, I have been able to live on unearned income.
For the collocations with *erzielen* see 3.2, Tricky translations, Exercise 2, p. 116.

[27] *sichern:* secure. For detailed explanations on the translations of 'sichern' see I.2.1, note [25], p. 17.

[28] *Wohlstand:* prosperity, wealth, also: affluence
'Affluence' *(Wohlstand, Reichtum, Überfluss)* often carries the connotation of having 'an overabundance of money or possessions' and is thus not quite appropriate here.

[29] *die damit verbundene höhere Motivation:* the stronger motivation that goes along with this; the increased motivation that this brings; the increase in motivation that results from this
For details on adverbial modifiers see XII.3.3, Exercise 2, p. 173

[30] *was zu ... führt:* leading to; resulting in; which leads to/results in

> Note the use of the gerund construction here.

3.1 Terminology: pay, performance and benefits

1 Complete the sentences using appropriate terms from the sample translation and the notes.

VIII.3 Exercises

1 An assembly worker can be remunerated by ___ ___ *(Stücklohn)*.
2 But for the growing number of 'knowledge workers' more complex ___ *(Vergütungs-)* systems are required, which ___ *(verknüpfen)* their own best interests to those of the company.
3 60% of our company's annual profits ___ ___ *(werden bezahlt)* to employees as ___-___ *(leistungsorientierte)* ___ *(Prämien)*.
4 The companies that do best in terms of shareholder returns are those that use a combination of ___ ___ *(variable Bezüge)* and fixed ___ *(Gehälter)*.

5 Tying pay to the ___ *(Erfolg)* of the business unit discourages excessive spending on ___ *(Zusatzvergünstigungen)*.

2 Supply an English term that could correspond to one of the meanings of *Zuwendung* in each of these sentences. Refer to the list in note [8], if necessary.

1 ___ provided by the employer such as medical insurance, company cars or interest-free loans must be declared for tax purposes.

2 Under our savings plan, the company pays a ___ of fifty cents for each dollar a participating employee contributes.

3 Without the government ___ that it has received in the last few years, the company would have gone bankrupt.

4 While she was studying, she received a regular ___ from her parents.

5 The firm gave all the staff a generous ___ at Christmas.

6 He received a small ___ from his aunt following her death last year.

7 Our institute is funded by ___ from private sources.

3.2 Tricky translations

1 Obtain and receive

Most people assume that 'obtain' and 'receive' are synonyms, because they can both be replaced by the ubiquitous colloquialism 'get' and can both be translated into German by *erhalten, bekommen* and other related verbs. Unfortunately this assumption is – in line with the English warning to be careful of using 'assume' because it makes an 'ass' out of 'u' and of 'me' – quite unfounded. Both verbs may well fit into the same sentence but they never have quite the same implication.

The verb 'to obtain' signifies 'to get (hold of) something by means of action or effort' or 'to get somebody to give you', whereas 'to receive' suggests simply that a person 'is the recipient of something'.

Virtually all synonyms of 'receive' are passive voice forms (e.g. 'is given') and ancillary constructions (e.g. 'get given') that have a passive voice character.

The following examples will elucidate the difference between the two verbs. Choose between them or take both. Make sure to adjust your choice to the syntax of the sentence (tense, gerund, aspect, etc.).

1 German students normally take, on average, five years ___ a university degree which they then ___ unceremoniously by post.
2 I ___ this information by looking at the company's website.
3 University graduates sometimes have difficulty in ___ a start-up loan for their intended business ventures.
4 They ___ the contract by outperforming their competitors.
5 The customer ___ / ___ the information she needed from the agency.
6 Before we pay we must make sure that we can ___ a receipt.
7 The driver ___ a warning from the police for parking his lorry on private premises.

Now translate the following synonyms of 'receive' *(erhalten)* using a passive voice construction. Include the words given in (brackets).

1 Jeder Mitarbeiter erhielt 10 Belegschaftsaktien. (allocate)
2 Wir erhielten Ihre Bewerbung per E-Mail. (send)
3 Letztes Jahr erhielten wir alle eine Gehaltserhöhung. (award)
4 Haben Sie schon Ihr Urlaubsgeld erhalten? (give; holiday pay)
5 Für diesen Verbesserungsvorschlag erhielt sie von dem Unternehmen einen Preis. (suggestion; award a prize)
6 Die Arbeiter erhalten ihren Bonus im Monat nach der Jahreshauptversammlung. (pay; annual general meeting)
7 Jeder Teilhaber erhält einen Gewinnanteil, der sich nach seinem Gehalt orientiert. (allocate)
8 Eine Leistungsprämie haben wir noch nicht erhalten. (give; performance bonus)
9 Er erhielt einen zusätzlichen Urlaubstag. (grant; extra day's leave)
10 Wir haben zu wenig Geld für das Werbeetat erhalten. (allocate; advertising budget)

2 *erzielen*

Please pick verbs from the box to translate *'erzielen'* and put them in an appropriate tense. There may be more than one option.

achieve • attain • fetch • have • make • meet with • obtain • reach • realise • yield

1 Our business unit ___ a profit of £20,000 last year.
2 At present, our customised products ___ high prices.
3 Most candidates ___ remarkable results.
4 A compromise was quickly ___.
5 We are proud to ___ such success.
6 This investment ___ substantial interest.
7 Work teams regularly ___ higher productivity rates.

3.3 Additional practice: reflexive verbs

Look at the following sentences. Which German reflexive verb is translated in each case?
1 We look forward to hearing from you soon
2 What is the letter about? It's about their order of 1 April.
3 When doing business in a foreign culture, it is important to know how to behave in certain situations.
4 I must get ready for the meeting now.
5 Were you bored at the lecture yesterday?

Now please translate the following sentences, using a dictionary if necessary.
1 Der Kunde beschwert sich über die verspätete Lieferung.
2 Falls Sie Schwierigkeiten mit der Bedienung des Geräts haben sollten, wenden Sie sich bitte an unseren Kundendienst.
3 Interessieren Sie sich für das Nachfolgemodell?
4 Wir würden uns sehr freuen, wenn ....
5 Ich fürchte, sie hat sich über deine Bemerkungen ziemlich geärgert.
6 Können wir uns gegen Ende des Monats treffen?
7 Ich muss sicher sein, daß ich mich auf diesen Termin verlassen kann.
8 Der Preis orientiert sich am Gewicht.
9 Die Verkaufszahlen haben sich verdoppelt, die Aufwendungen haben sich halbiert.

IX Process Management

IX Process Management

Anmerkung: Der folgende Textauszug zeigt die Umsetzung einer übergeordneten TQM-Strategie im Bereich der Produktion at John Deere Werke Mannheim (JDWM).

(IDS Scheer)

Die Bedeutung des Produktentwicklungsprozesses

Der Begriff „Product Delivery Process" (PDP) steht seit einigen Jahren innerhalb unseres Unternehmens für eine Initiative, die die Entwicklung neuer Produkte als einen Prozess versteht, den es sorgfältig zu gestalten gilt. Dies ist weniger eine Aufgabe der funktionalen Organisation, sondern vielmehr eine, die das gesamte Werk, und in bestimmten Entwicklungsphasen auch externe Stellen, mit einbezieht.

Die Neugestaltung der Produktentwicklung hat verschiedene Ursachen:

- Die Marktsituation lässt nicht mehr die frühere, durch die Betonung der Funktionalorganisation bedingte sequenzielle Abarbeitung von Entwicklungsprojekten zu, die die Entwicklungsdauer übermäßig verlängerte. Das Unternehmen ist heute gezwungen, nicht nur „gut", sondern auch „schnell" zu entwickeln. Dies lässt sich nur durch möglichst parallele Bearbeitung und fertigungssynchrone Beschaffung in den einzelnen Fabrikbereichen realisieren. Diese Vorgehensweise, die auch als „Simultaneous Engineering" bekannt ist, erfordert Prozesse, die eine rechtzeitige Querinformation innerhalb der Bereiche sowie eine Koordination aller Aktivitäten zwischen den Bereichen ermöglichen.
- Die modernen EDV-Systeme erleichtern und erzwingen eine weitgehende Vernetzung von F&E Aktivitäten, Marketing und den produzierenden Bereichen.
- Die Entwicklung der „richtigen" Produkte bestimmt in Zukunft den Unternehmenserfolg. Finanzielle Mittel für mögliche Fehlentwicklungen stehen nicht zur Verfügung. Daher muss der Entwicklungsprozess dazu führen, dass die Fabrik als Einheit die richtigen produktbezogenen Entscheidungen rechtzeitig trifft und somit die Weichen für den künftigen Erfolg stellt.

Die Darstellung des Produktentwicklungsprozesses
Die Produktentwicklung umfasst alle zur Entwicklung neuer Produkte gehörenden Aktivitäten innerhalb der JDWM, d.h. unter anderem:

- alle Denkanstöße und Vorschläge
- die verschiedenen Definitionsphasen
- die schrittweise Realisierung des Produktionsprozesses und die Erprobung des Produktes, die alle internen (z. B. Schwestergesellschaften) und externen (z. B. Lieferanten) Stellen der Produktentwicklung mit einbezieht
- die Veränderung der bestehenden Produktpalette unter Berücksichtigung des Marktes, der Konkurrenz und des neuesten Technologiestandes
- die Produktionsreife des neuen Produktes.

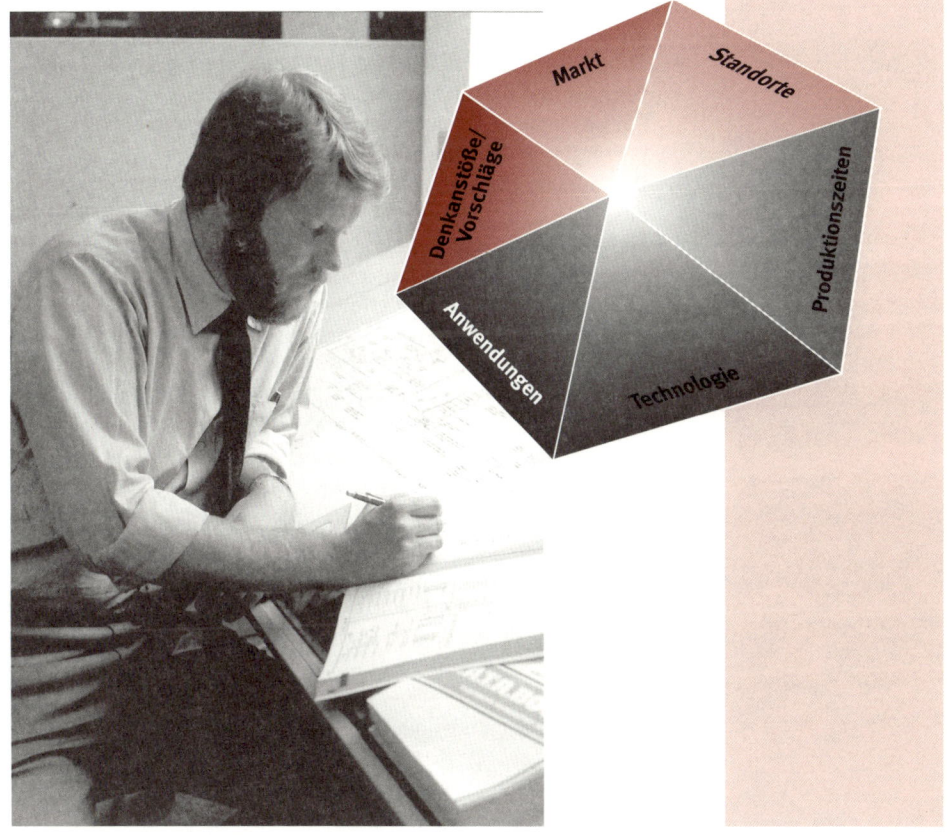

Der PDP der Agriculture Division (AG) wurde in einem vorausgegangenem Projekt an die Rahmenbedingungen der JDWM angepasst und umgesetzt. Doch die Implementierung zeigte, dass die Darstellungsform des Prozesses verschiedene Schwachstellen bezüglich der Transparenz des zeitlichen Ablaufes, der funktionalen Verbindungen zu den einzelnen Prozessschritten sowie der den einzelnen Mitarbeitern zugewiesenen Funktionen aufwies. Auch Kunden- und Lieferantenbeziehungen (extern und intern) waren nicht immer nachvollziehbar.

Daraus resultierten Informationslücken und Terminverschiebungen.

Aus diesen Erfahrungen wurden folgende Prozessziele abgeleitet

- Der Entwicklungsprozess soll in zeitlicher Abfolge dargestellt werden
- Die Beziehungen zwischen den einzelnen Prozessschritten sollen aufgezeigt werden
- Subprozesse und zuständige Funktionsbereiche sollen gekennzeichnet und benannt werden

Die besonderen Eigenschaften des überarbeiteten Entwicklungsprozesses sind im folgenden zusammengefasst:

- Der Produktentwicklungsprozess (PDP) soll so dargestellt werden, dass er als Gesamtwerkzeug zur Prozessanalyse und Prozessverbesserung dient. Deshalb beinhaltet die Darstellungsform des Prozesses alle Informationen, die für ein optimales Projekt- und Informationsmanagement erforderlich sind.
- Allgemein zielt der Prozess auf ein Höchstmaß der Kundenzufriedenheit mit dem neuen Produkt und gleichzeitig auf ein Höchstmaß an Rentabilität. Die Prozessdarstellung soll Projektteam und Management in die Lage versetzen, über alle Phasen der Produktentwicklung hinweg, permanent das Erreichen der Ziele des Entwicklungsprojektes zu verfolgen bzw. die Erreichbarkeit dieser Ziele einzuschätzen. Außerdem sollen sie auftretende Probleme so rechtzeitig erkennen können, dass differenzierte Gegenmaßnahmen eingeleitet werden können.
- Die Prozessdarstellung soll es ermöglichen, alle Potentiale der Prozessbeschleunigung bzw. der Verkürzung der Entwicklungsdauer auszuschöpfen.

(Text provided by J. Kreienbaum, Process Manager, JDWM)

Product Delivery Process

Note: The following excerpt **demonstrates**[1] the implementation of a **superordinate**[2] **Total Quality Management**[3] strategy in production at John Deere Werke Mannheim (JDWM).

Significance of the Product Delivery Process[4]

In the past few years, the term "Product Delivery Process" has stood for an initiative in our company **which defines the development** of new products **as**[5] a process **that needs to be designed with great care**[6]. This is less a task of the **functional organisation**[7] than one **that involves the entire company**[8] – as well as, at certain development stages, the **external partners**[9].

There are several reasons for the restructuring of product development.

- The **current market**[10] no longer permits the formerly employed **sequential processing**[11] of development projects, **which was due to the emphasis on**[12] the functional organisation and **unduly prolonged**[13] the development phase. Nowadays, an enterprise **is forced**[14] not only to develop "well" but also to develop "fast". The only way to achieve this is **by establishing the highest possible degree of concurrent processing**[15] and by **JIT purchasing**[16] in the individual manufacturing sectors. This **approach**[17], also known as **simultaneous engineering**[18] – requires processes which not only allow **timely cross-departmental communication**[19] but also permit the co-ordination of all inter-departmental activities.
- Modern EDP systems both **facilitate and demand**[20] an **extensive interaction**[21] between **R & D**[22], marketing and the producing areas.
- In future, the development of the right products will be the decisive factor behind corporate success. There are no financial resources for potentially **deficient development procedures**[23]. For this reason, the development process has to ensure that the factory takes the right product-related decisions at the right time, **thereby paving the way for future success**[24].

Mapping[25] the Product Delivery Process

- Product development comprises all activities necessary for the development of new products at JDWM, i.e. among other things:
- all **conceptual ideas**[26] and suggestions
- the various phases of definition

- **the step-by-step implementation of the production process**[27] and product testing including all the internal (e.g. **sister companies**[28]) and the external (e.g. suppliers) partners involved in product development
- the alteration of the current product range **taking into account**[29] the market, the competitors and the **state-of-the-art technology**[30]
- **production maturity**[31] of the new product

The PDP of the agricultural division was **aligned with the JDWM framework**[32] and implemented in a previous project. In the course of the implementation, however, it became apparent that the way in which the process was mapped contained several **flaws**[33] regarding the **clarity**[34] of the **time schedule**[35], the functional links between the individual process steps and the tasks assigned to individual employees. Moreover, internal and external customer and/or supplier relations were not **traceable**[36]. This led to information gaps and **delays**[37].

Based on this experience, the following process goals were **arrived at**[38]:

- PDP is to be mapped chronologically
- The interrelations between the individual steps of the process are to be indicated.
- Sub-processes and the functional areas they belong to **are to be identified and named**[39].

  The specific features of the revised development process are summed up in the following:
- PDP should be mapped in a manner that makes it **a generally applicable tool**[40] for process analysis and process improvement. It therefore contains all information which optimal project and information management requires.
- The process generally **aims at the highest possible degree of customer satisfaction**[41] with the new product as well the highest possible degree of profitability. Process mapping should **place the project team** and the management **in a position**[42] to continuously pursue their goals through all phases of the development project and/or **to assess the attainability of these goals**[43]. **Moreover**[44], they should be enabled **to detect**[45] problems which occur in the process **in time**[46] to take **targeted countermeasures**[47].
- Process mapping **is designed to**[48] make it possible to exploit all potential ways of speeding up the development process and/or of shortening the development phase.

2.1 Notes on the translation

1   *zeigt:* demonstrates; is an example of

2   *übergeordnete:* superordinate
The term comprises the corporate strategies that are based on the company's shared values. See V.2.1, note [18], p. 71.

3   Total Quality Management, TQM: *(allumfassendes) Qualitäts-management; ganzheitliches Qualitätsmanagement*

← Please note

> 'TQM' is strongly influenced by the Japanese *Kaizen* (literal translation: 'always seeking to find the right way') philosophy of steadily trying to perfect the way in which a person handles his/her life. 'TQM' strategies therefore replace 'close enough' attitudes in business by a 'get it right first time' and a 'prevent instead of mend' approach. 'TQM' aims at covering the 'totality' of people and methods involved in a process. It realises that most errors lie in the flawed processes themselves and therefore aims at improving all process variables. It is intent on eradicating all non-value adding stages from business processes and on eliminating all types of waste (time, motion, transportation, inventory). It has engendered a series of restructuring strategies such as 'Business Process Reengineering' (VII.2.1, note [27], p. 99), 'Simultaneous Engineering' (note [18], p. 125) and 'JIT deliveries' (note [16], p. 125).

4   *Produktentwicklungsprozess:* Product Delivery Process (PDP); product development process
'Product Delivery Process' (PDP) is the official term used by the John Deere group. It is an optimised product development process which is 'mandatory' *(verbindlich)* for all divisions.

5   *die die Entwicklung ... versteht als:* which defines the development as; which regards / perceives the development as

6   *den es sorgfältig zu gestalten gilt:* that needs to be designed with great care; which needs to be structured very carefully
'Product design' *(Konzipierung, Konstruktion)* not only comprises the physical appearance of a product but also the organisation of the production process.

7   *funktionale Organisation:* functional organisation

← Please note

> A 'functional organisation' is structured according to its individual business functions (production, finance, HRM, marketing, etc.) which contribute their share to the overall organisation. The 'management function' co-ordinates these

contributions in order to optimise their effectiveness. However, in practice, this has failed to maximise synergy. Consequently, the approach favoured by companies such as John Deere seeks to encompass a much wider range of know-how and expertise.

8   *die das ganze Werk mit einbezieht:* that involves the entire company; which engages/integrates the whole corporation

> *Werk* here is a collective term for all units involved in the process of manufacturing agricultural equipment (synonym: *Betrieb*).
> *Werk/Werke* also translates 'works' (which is polysemous and often functions as a singular noun). 'Works' denotes 'a place where something is produced', a 'factory' or 'site' but also a 'mechanism' of a machine or instrument.
> Usage examples
> works council: *Betriebsrat*
> the gas works nearby: *die Gaswerke/das Gaswerk hier in der Nähe*
> to put the spanner in the works: *Sand ins Getriebe streuen*
> the works of a clock: *ein Uhrwerk*
> road works: *Baustelle, Bauarbeiten*
> the works of Shakespeare: *Shakespeares Werk(e)*

9   *externe Stellen:* external partners
Stelle carries a large variety of meanings. In this context, it it is an all-inclusive term for all partners and units contributing to the production process, but it may also denote a 'vacancy to be filled' *(freie Stelle)* or 'a branch office' *(Außenstelle).*

10 *die Marktsituation:* the current market; the marketplace (US)
More literal translations of *Marktsituation* would be 'the current situation in the market' and 'the current market situation'.

11 *sequenzielle Abarbeitung:* sequential processing; step-by-step processing

12 *die durch die Betonung bedingte:* which was due to the emphasis on; which resulted/arose from the emphasis on

13 *übermäßig verlängert:* unduly prolonged; unduly/unnecessarily extended; made ... (much) longer than necessary

14 *ist gezwungen:* is forced; is compelled

15 *durch möglichst parallele Bearbeitung:* by establishing the highest possible degree of/level of concurrent processing

> It is possible to translate the prepositive modifier *möglichst* as a paraphrase, namely *wo immer dies in der Herstellung möglich ist:* 'wherever/whenever this is possible in manufacturing.' This adjectival phrase can be interjected in the main sentence or added to it.

See also XII.3.3, Exercise 2, p. 173.

[16] *fertigungssynchrone Beschaffung, beständelose Beschaffung;* just in time purchasing; JIT purchasing

← Please note

> 'Just in Time' (JIT) is a widely-applied approach in the production sectors. It tackles 'bottlenecks' *(Engpässe)*, 'overproduction' *(Überproduktion)* and 'financial resources tied up' *(Kapitalbindung)* in factory space and warehousing by establishing a 'demand pull' *(Nachfragesog)* system according to which goods are only 'produced on order' *(Auftragsproduktion)* and material only flows into the production process when and where it is immediately required.
> The downside of JIT is higher fuel consumption, fuel prices, congested roads and road tolls.

> The pronunciation of JIT is J:I:T. Cf. also V:I:P, which in English is never pronounced as 'Vip' (as it is in German).

[17] *Vorgehensweise:* approach; procedure; method
[18] simultaneous engineering: *simultane Produktion*

← Please note

> 'Simultaneous engineering', also known as 'concurrent engineering' *(parallele Produktion)* and 'interactive engineering' *(vernetzte Produktion)*, aims at shortening the 'lead times' *(Laufzeiten)* in production by arranging the production process in task-oriented and multilevel cells and stages.

[19] *eine rechtzeitige Querinformation innerhalb der Bereiche:* timely cross-departmental communication

> Information signifies, firstly 'a piece of information' which is communicated, and secondly (as in the above text), 'transfer of information' or 'communication process'.

[20] *erleichtern und erzwingen:* facilitate and demand; facilitate and necessitate

•••••••• 21 *weitgehende Vernetzung:* extensive interaction

> *Vernetzung* cannot be translated as 'networking' as this signifies 'establishing and exploiting the right connections'.

22 *F & E; Forschung & Entwicklung:* Research & Development; R & D

Please note →

> R & D is a vital function in manufacturing and the IT industries. It focuses on innovative products and procedures, short development cycles, product and process improvement. Owing to its cost-intensive nature, basic research is almost exclusively conducted by major corporations.

23 *mögliche Fehlentwicklungen:* potentially deficient development procedures; potentially flawed development

24 *und somit die Weichen für den künftigen Erfolg stellt:* thereby paving the way for future success; thus laying the foundations for

> The railway term 'to set the points' cannot be used metaphorically like *die Weichen stellen*. However, the two alternative metaphors suggested here carry the same semantic message.
> The related expression 'to put a person on the right track' means *jemand auf die richtige Fährte setzen*, i.e. 'to show him/her a successful line of investigation'.

For further practice on *somit, dabei* and similar constructions see VI.3.3. Exercise 2, p. 88.

25 *Darstellung:* mapping
'Mapping' denotes the way in which the process is visualized and presented.
If this presentation is integrated into a graph, 'plotting' would also be appropriate.
Example
The curve plots the development of our current production rates.

26 *Denkanstöße:* conceptual ideas, rough concepts, suggestions

27 *die schrittweise Realisierung des Produktionsprozesses:* the step-by-step implementation of the production process; the incremental realisation of the production phase
'Product testing' can also include the 'trial run' *(Probelauf)* of a machine.

28 *Schwestergesellschaften:* sister companies
These organisations form part of one group and are organised in an identical fashion.

29   *unter Berücksichtigung von:* taking into account/into consideration

    See also Exercise 3.3 below, p. 130.

30   *des neuesten Technologiestandes:* state-of-the-art technology; most advanced level of technology

31   *Produktionsreife:* production maturity

    This is the phase in which production can be started on a larger scale.

32   *an die Rahmenbedingungen der JDWM angepasst:* aligned with the JDWM framework; adapted to the JDWM framework

33   *Schwachstellen:* flaws; deficiencies; weaknesses

    For detailed explanations concerning the term 'deficiency' and for synonymous expressions see XI.2.1, note [28], p. 152.

34   *Transparenz:* clarity

> Note that 'transparency' is sometimes a false friend. It may signify that something is easy to see through, but very often it is synonymous with 'slide': *Präsentationsfolie, Dia.*

35   *zeitlicher Ablauf:* time schedule; chronological order

36   *waren nicht nachvollziehbar:* were not traceable; could not be traced; were not clear; were not clearly apparent

37   *Terminverschiebungen:* delays; hold-ups; postponed dates

38   *abgeleitet:* arrived at; derived

39   *sollen gekennzeichnet und benannt werden:* are to be identified and named; are to be highlighted/labelled/marked and named

40   *ein Gesamtwerkzeug:* a generally applicable tool; a commonly applicable/an all-purpose instrument

41   *ein Höchstmaß an Kundenzufriedenheit:* the highest possible degree of/level of customer satisfaction

42   *das Projektteam in die Lage versetzen:* place the project team in a position; enable the project team; put the project team in a position

43   *die Erreichbarkeit der Ziele einschätzen:* to assess the attainability of these goals; to assess the chances of attaining these aims

44   *außerdem:* moreover; furthermore; in addition

45   *erkennen:* to detect; to identify; to spot; to pinpoint

46   *so rechtzeitig:* in time

> 'In time' is followed by an infinitive or by a prepositional object, e.g. 'for something'.

Examples
just in time for assembly
just in time to be assembled

[47] *differenzierte Gegenmaßnahmen:* targeted countermeasures; appropriate countermeasures

> *Differenziert* means *zielgerichtet*, i.e. 'targeted'. Such measures differ from the ordinary response to problems in so far as they are 'more thought over' and 'specifically tailored to' the problem they are to solve.
> 'Differentiated' would NOT be correct in this context.

[48] *soll:* is designed to; is to
See also VI.3.3 Additional practice p. 86.

IX.3 Exercises

3.1 Terminology: processes and problems

1 Fill the gaps using the terms and expressions provided in the notes.

1 The functional organisation with its linear hierarchy and rigid compartmentalisation has often ___ *(versäumt)* to ___ *(hervorbringen)* the synergy effects required in contemporary businesses.

2 JIT is said to transfer the warehouses to the roads, which are becoming more and more ___ *(verstopft)*. As a result, the introduction of ___ *(gebührenpflichtige Straßen)* is now very much on the agenda.

3 The TQM principle demands that all types of waste occurring in a business process should be ___ *(von Grund auf beseitigt; ausgemerzt)* and rejects all ___ ___ *(Das ist gut genug!)* attitudes.

4 ___ *(in Einklang bringen)* the cost-cutting measures executed on the shopfloor to / with the ___ *(übergeordnete)* corporate strategy may present a problem.

5 TQM requires proactive rather than reactive behaviour and processes with designed-in error ___ *(Erkennung)* and ___ *(Vorbeugung)*.

6 The specific ___ *(Vorzüge)* of the revised process are its ___ *(Transparenz)* and its common ___ *(Anwendbarkeit)* which allows the management to constantly assess the ___ *(Erreichbarkeit)* of the set goals.

7 We have prepared several ___ *(Folien)* which will serve to visualise the intricate nature of this process.

8 ___ *(vernetzte)* and ___ *(vielschichtige)* processes shorten the product ___ *(Laufzeiten)*.

9 Product development was impeded by several ___ ___ *(Konstruktionsfehlern)*.

2 Problems are often pictured as 'controversial issues', which cannot be resolved, 'dangerous situations', which have to be mastered, or 'predicaments' *(missliche Situationen)*, which we find ourselves in. They are likened to 'hurdles' and 'obstacles', that need to be overcome, to 'uphill struggles', which we are facing, to 'tall orders', which present a major challenge, or to 'thin ice', on which we feel unsafe. Some of these metaphors are universal; others, such as the proverbial 'sticky wicket', are uniquely British.

Find the verbs that collocate with 'problem'.
1 Problems can frequently ___ *(vorkommen, auftreten)* or suddenly ___ *(auftauchen)*.
2 They can ___ *(vorausgesehen werden)* or ___ *(übersehen werden)*.
3 We can try to ___ *(ignorieren)* them, hoping that they will ___ *(verschwinden)*, or we can decide to ___ *(in Angriff nehmen/sich vornehmen)* them.
4 Hurdles can be ___ *(übersprungen)*; obstacles can be ___ *(überwunden)* or ___ *(zur Seite geräumt)*.
5 Tricky issues may ___ *(gelöst werden)* or ___ ___ *(ungelöst beleiben)*.
6 Problems can be ___ *(knifflig)*, or ___ *(kinderleicht)*.

Please translate the following English idioms.
1 This sounds like a tall order.
2 You are facing an uphill struggle.
3 We got ourselves in a tight spot.
4 We have no leeway when it comes to prices.

Please translate the following German phrases.
5 Da liegt der Hase begraben!
6 Vorbeugen ist besser als Heilen.
7 Sie reagierten erst, als das Kind in den Brunnen gefallen war.
8 Wir sind vom Regen in die Traufe gekommen.

3.2 Tricky translations: process management

Translate the sentences below. Use the suggestions made in (brackets).

1 Prozessmanagement setzt voraus, daß alle betrieblichen Abläufe sorgfältig geplant und gestaltet werden. (presupposes)

2 Technologisch gesehen, sollen diese Prozesse den höchsten Entwicklungsstand reflektieren (mirror).

3 Die Prozessplanung soll ein nützliches Gesamtwerkzeug darstellen. (represent)

4 Überschaubare Prozesse sind leichter umsetzbar.

5 Schwestergesellschaften und Außenstellen sind in diesen Prozess einbezogen.

6 Diese Art von Prozessdarstellung sollte entweder auf Eis gelegt (shelved) oder ganz verworfen werden (scrapped).

7 Prozessmanagement hat zu gewährleisten, dass Mängel vermieden werden.

8 Die im Unternehmen vorhandene breite Palette an Fachwissen und Erfahrungen soll dem Prozess zugute kommen.

9 Arbeitszeit-, Material-, Energieverschwendung treiben die Produktionskosten in die Höhe.

3.3 Additional practice: more adverbials

Translate the following adverbials which link or contrast statements with the help of the list below and the clues given in German. Some adverbials can be employed in more than one sentence.

according to • as a result of • as far as … is concerned • as to • due to • because of • by contrast • by way of introduction • compared to • in contrast to • in the course of • in the wake of • in this respect • in view of • owing to • taking … into account • taking into consideration • thanks to • unlike • with regard to

1 Production output exceeded all our expectations. Sales, ___ ___ , plummeted to an overall low. *(im Gegensatz dazu)*

2 ___ last year, the goals seem to be more easily attainable. *(im Vergleich zu)*

3 ___ the deutschmark (DEM), the euro did not appreciate against the pound sterling (GBP). *(im Unterschied / Gegensatz zu)*

4 Prices rose last year, ___ wages. *(im Gegensatz zu)*

5 ___ the new calculations, it was decided to outsource the production of the standardized parts. *(unter Berücksichtigung der)*

6 ___ the low turnover, the toy factory was closed. *(wegen)*

7 ___ TQM, corporate life has changed beyond recognition. *(dank)*

8 Productivity increased ___ interactive engineering. *(infolge von)*

9 This decision was taken ___ the current developments in the global market. *(im Hinblick auf)*

10 ___ our suggestion, we would be interested to know your views on this topic. *(was ... anbelangt)*

11 ___, the measures taken seem adequate. *(in dieser Hinsicht)*

12 ___ the negotiations, the major hurdles were removed. *(im Verlauf der)*

13 ___ I would like to point out that we are happy about the overall development of our new subsidiary. *(einleitend)*

14 ___ the British Press, the number of unemployed is currently declining. *(laut)*

15 ___ our contract, payment is due within 30 days after delivery. *(in Übereinstimmung mit/gemäß)*

X Enquiry Agencies and Debt Collectors

X Enquiry Agencies and Debt Collectors

Wenn Hersteller, Dienstleister und Händler grenzübergreifende Geschäfte tätigen, stellt sich ihnen zwangsläufig die Frage nach der Zahlungsmoral ihrer ausländischen Kunden. Vor allem britische Firmen scheinen beim pünktlichen Bezahlen schlechter abzuschneiden als ihre europäischen Nachbarn.

Aus diesem Grund erleben Auskunfteien und Inkassobüros derzeit einen starken Aufschwung. Ironischerweise, erschwert gerade der technische Fortschritt die Überwachung internationaler Geschäfte, einerseits wegen der großen Anzahl der täglichen Geschäftsabschlüsse und andererseits wegen der Schnelligkeit, mit der die Computer Aufträge bearbeiten und die versandten Waren noch vor ihrer Auslieferung in Rechnungen stellen können.

Viele Geschäftsleute sehen sich daher veranlasst, sich an Auskunfteien, Kreditanstalten und selbst an langjährige Geschäftspartner zu wenden, um verläßliche Auskünfte über künftige Partner zu erhalten. Der Bericht der Auskunftei enthält Angaben über den Ruf und die Geschäftsfähigkeit potentieller Kunden oder Darlehensnehmer, ihre finanziellen Verbindlichkeiten und Forderungen, ihre Zahlungsfähigkeit, finanziellen Ressourcen und Finanzierungsmöglichkeiten sowie über ihr bevorzugtes Geschäftsgebaren.

Darüber hinaus geben die Banken den Firmen Empfehlungen über die Angemessenheit der von Kunden gewüschten Zahlungs- und Lieferbedingungen.

(M. Seidenspinner)

A booming business[1] for enquiry agencies[2] and commercial collection services[3]

Whenever manufacturers, service providers and **distributors**[4] conduct cross-border business, they are **inevitably**[5] confronted with the question as to the payment morale of their foreign customers. British companies, in particular, **seem to perform worse** than their European neighbours **when it comes to paying punctually**[6]. This is why enquiry agencies and debt collection agencies are currently **experiencing a boom**[7]. Ironically enough, it is technological progress itself which **hampers**[8] the **monitoring**[9] of international **business transactions**[10]. On the one hand, this is due to the high number of commercial deals that are concluded every day and, on the other, to the speed with which computers can process **orders**[11] and produce invoices for the consignments dispatched even before delivery has been effected.

As a result, a lot of business people **see no alternative but**[12] to turn to enquiry agencies, credit institutions and **even**[13] to **long-standing**[14] business partners in order to obtain reliable information about their prospective partners.

The enquiry report **contains**[15] information about the reputation of potential **customers**[16] or borrowers and their **capacity to contract**[17], about their financial **liabilities and debtors**[18], their **solvency**[19], **financial resources**[20] and **the financing available**[21] as well as about their **preferred business methods**[22]. In addition, banks advise companies about the **suitability**[23] of the **terms of payment and delivery**[24] demanded by customers.

2.1 Notes on the translation

[1] *im Aufwind:* a booming business; a roaring trade; soaring profits
[2] *Auskunfteien:* enquiry agencies; also spelt: 'inquiry'
[3] *Inkassobüros:* commercial collection services; debt collection agencies; debt recovery agencies

← Please note

> An organisation that is commissioned to recover the money due to its clients, such as 'overdue receivables' (see note [18] below, p. 139) within an agreed 'collection period'. Originally, these agencies were known as 'debt collectors', a term which is now considered to be offensive and dated. 'Commercial collection agencies' work on a commission basis (see note [4], p. 136).

●●●●●●●● Related expressions

debt counselling: *Schuldenberatung*

debt restructuring, debt rescheduling: *Umschuldung*

debt reduction, debt relief: *Schuldenerlass*

debt servicing: *Schuldendienst*, i.e. 'the repayment of an existing debt including the interest incurred'.

Common collocations

to incur debts: *Schulden machen*

to repay the debts: *die Schulden zurückzahlen*

to settle the debts: *die Schulden begleichen*

to accumulate debts: *Schulden anhäufen*

to pay off the debts: *die Schulden abzahlen*

to honour debts: *die Schulden zahlen (eigentlich zu seinen Schulden stehen)*

[4] *Händler:* distributor, dealer

Please note →

- *Einzelhändler:* retailer
- *Großhändler:* wholesaler
- *Direkthändler:* 'dealers' who acquire ownership of the goods they buy from the manufacturer. Like retailers and wholesalers, they are granted a 'mark-up' *(Handelsaufschlag)* on the sales or wholesale price but no commission.
- *Vertragshändler:* 'distributors' also 'concessionaires' who either work for one manufacturer (as a 'dealer') or for a limited number of businesses (as a 'wholesaler'). They usually focus on certain areas or products.
- *Handelsvertreter:* 'commercial agents'. These are persons who represent an organisation or an individual business person but who act in their own name and at their own cost. They usually work on a 'commission basis' *(Provisionsbasis)*: they receive a percentage of the amount they sell.

False friends

Examples

'Provisions' can mean – among other things – *Rückstellungen, Wertberichtigungen, (Vertrags)bestimmungen, Vorkehrungen* or *Vorräte*. 'Commission' may translate *Auftrag* (see I.2.1, note [13], p. 14) or *Provision*.

Diese Dienstleistung ist provisionsfrei. This service is free of commission. *Die ersten Legobausteine wurden auf Kommissionsbasis vertrieben.* The first Lego bricks were distributed on a sale or return basis.

5   *zwangsläufig:* inevitably ...; are bound to be ...

6   *scheinen beim pünktlichen Bezahlen schlechter abzuschneiden:* seem to perform worse ... when it comes to paying punctually; appear to perform worse as far as punctual payments are concerned

7   *einen starken Aufschwung erleben:* to experience a boom; to enjoy a booming/flourishing/prospering trade
Alternatively: 'This is why business is booming for enquiry agencies ...'

← Please note

> - Trade can be 'steady' *(gleichbleibend)* or 'stagnating'; it can be 'slow', 'slack' *(lasch)* or 'sluggish' *(träge)*.
> - Trade can 'shrink' *(rückläufig sein)* or 'stop'; it can 'recover' (i.e. 'pick up') and 'prosper' *(gedeihen, blühen)* again.
> - Trade figures may 'hover around' *(sich um ... bewegen)* a certain level or 'fluctuate'; they can 'increase', 'go up', 'soar', 'shoot up' *(in die Höhe schießen)* or 'rocket sky high'. By contrast, they can 'decrease', 'drop', 'fall', 'plummet', 'plunge' or 'nosedive' *(abstürzen)*.

8   *behindert:* hampers; impedes; hinders

9   *Überwachung:* monitoring; supervision

10 *Geschäfte:* business transactions; business deals; commercial deals
See 3.1, Exercise 2, p. 141

11 *Auftrag:* order
'Order' has multiple semantic aspects. In the above text it signifies:

← Please note

> - *Bestellung*, i.e. firstly, the 'commission to produce and/or supply a commercial item in return for payment', and secondly, the 'goods ordered' and the 'order form'.
> Examples
> They have placed an order for 20 generators.
> Has the order been shipped yet?
> I am looking for Mr. Downing's order.
> There are several types of orders:
> *Erstaufträge:* initial orders, first orders
> *Wiederholungsaufträge:* repeat orders
> *Einzelaufträge:* single orders
> *Großaufträge:* bulk orders, large-scale orders (colloquial: big tickets)

••••••••

Sammelbestellungen: joint orders, collective orders
unerledigte Aufträge: back orders
'Order backlogs' are *Auftragsrückstände*; *Fehlbestände* are 'stockouts'.
In addition, 'order' may signify:

- *Ordnung:* states a well-established rule, an arranged succession or sequence, e.g. in 'order of business' *(Tagesordnung)* which determines when the items on the agenda are dealt with.
  Further examples
  in alphabetical/chronological order: *in alphabetischer/zeitlicher Reihenfolge*
  in order of excellence: *nach Qualitätsgrad geordnet*
  This is our itemized breakdown of figures but we need not discuss it in this order. *in dieser Reihenfolge*
  This is the customer's order of preference: *die vom Kunden bevorzugte Reihenfolge*
  Flocks of fowl usually adhere to their pecking order: *Hackordnung*
- *Verfügung:* a directive or an instruction by a court or a governmental body.
- *Befehl:* a command, an instruction that must be obeyed.
- *Anweisung:* see I.2.1, note [13], p. 14; for the collocations of 'order' see 3.1, Exercise 2, p. 141.

[12] *sehen sich veranlasst:* see no alternative but to …; see themselves forced to

[13] *selbst:* even
For further usage examples of *selbst* (i.e. *sogar*) see XII.3.3 Additional practice, Exercise 1, p. 172.

[14] *langjährig:* long-standing

'Long-term' *(langfristig)* would be inappropriate here. It refers to (mostly future) relations or agreements which are intended to extend over a specified period of time.

[15] *enthält:* contains; includes; comprises

Please note →

Note the difference between 'include' and 'comprise'
The 'SOHO' (small office, home office) sector also includes people who work in very small organisations. (amongst other people)

> The SME sector comprises small and medium-sized companies.
> (both elements make up the whole sector)
> Note the related term 'consist of': *bestehen aus*.
> Example
> This sand consists of 90 per cent quartz.

● ● ● ● ● ● ● ●

[16] *Kunden:* customers. See III.2.1, note [23], p. 47.

[17] *Geschäftsfähigkeit:* capacity to contract; contractual capacity

[18] *Verbindlichkeiten und Forderungen:* liabilities and debtors; accounts payable and receivable (US); also: trade creditors and trade debtors (GB); trade payables and trade receivables

> • In corporate balance sheets, 'liabilities' (in its broader sense) form part of the Passiva, which consist of 'equity & liabilities'. These are broken down into
> *Eigenkapital:* equity
> *Rückstellungen:* provisions/accrued liabilities
> *Verbindlichkeiten:* liabilities – in its narrower sense
> The latter include, for instance: 'loans' and 'liabilities to banks' *(Anleihen, Verbindlichkeiten gegenüber Kredit-instituten)*, 'creditors'/'trade payables' *(Verbindlichkeiten aus Lieferungen und Leistungen)*, 'advance payments on orders' *(Anzahlungen auf Bestellungen)*, 'bills of exchange payable' *(Wechselverbindlichkeiten)* as well as other 'amounts payable to group and affiliated undertakings' *(Verbindlichkeiten gegenüber verbundenen oder assoziier-ten Unternehmen)*.
> • *Forderungen* are 'outstanding amounts' or 'uncollected receivables'. They may be: 'trade debtors' *(Forderungen aus Lieferungen und Leistungen)*, 'bills of exchange receivables' *(Wechselforderungen)*, 'specific and general provisions' *(Einzelwert- und Pauschalwertberichtigungen)* as well as amounts owed from group and associated undertakings.
> Further usage examples
> irrecoverable debts: *uneinbringliche Forderungen*
> waived debts: *Forderungsverzicht*
> In the balance sheet, *Forderungen* form part of a company's 'current assets' (see VIII, note [4], p. 107).

← Please note

[19] *Zahlungsfähigkeit:* solvency

> 'Solvency' indicates that a company is 'financially sound', i.e. it possesses sufficient 'liquid assets' to discharge its financial

← Please note

obligations or can acquire such assets at short notice by converting current corporate assets into cash. This ability is also referred to as 'liquidity'.

The opposite of 'liquidity' and 'solvency' is 'insolvency' *(Zahlungsunfähigkeit).*
A colloquial English expression to describe a lack of financial funds is 'to be in dire financial straits' *(finanzieller Engpass).*

[20] *finanzielle Ressourcen:* financial resources; financial means

Note the different spelling of 'resources' in English.

[21] *Finanzierungsmöglichkeiten:* the financing available
This includes the availability of working capital for the everyday business as well as of investment capital and/or loans.
[22] *ihr bevorzugtes Geschäftsgebaren:* their preferred business methods; the business approach they favour
Note that 'preferable' means *vorzuziehend/e.*
[23] *Angemessenheit:* suitability; appropriateness
[24] *Zahlungs- und Lieferbedingungen:* terms of payment and delivery
For payment methods in international trade see chapter XI, p. 146.

3.1 Terminology: trading and ordering

1 Please fill in the gaps below. Take the terms from the sample translation and the notes.

1 Very much to our dismay, the deal was ___ *(abgeschlossen)* before we were able to ___ ___ *(Auskunft einholen)* about the company's ___ *(Zahlungsfähigkeit)*.

2 Our ___ *(Handelsvertreter)* is paid a ___ *(Provision)* of 10 per cent of the sales price.

3 The car ___ *(Händler)* enjoys a good reputation with his customers.

4 Our ___ *(Vertragshändler)* sells directly to the ___ *(Endverbraucher)* as well as to the local ___ *(Einzelhändler)*.

5 In Japan it is not uncommon for business people to _____ *(gründen)* a business in ___ *(Großhandel)* after retirement in order to supplement their pension.

6 The ___ *(Zahlungs- und Lieferbedingungen)* are the specific conditions agreed between a ___ *(Käufer)* and a ___ *(Verkäufer)* according to which shipment of the ___ *(Handelsware)* is carried out and ___ *(Zahlung)* is finalized.

7 The former is also referred to as the ___ *(Zahlender)* whereas the latter is known as the ___ *(Zahlungsempfänger)*.

2 Orders
Consult your dictionaries to find the suitable collocation for the following activities which are all connected to 'order' in the sense of *'Bestellung'* and *'Auftrag'*. They are arranged in the 'order' in which they usually occur in business processes.

eine Bestellung erhalten	to receive an order
1 den Auftragseingang bestätigen	___
2 den Auftrag bestätigen	___
3 die Bestellung abheften/abspeichern	___
4 den Auftrag weiterleiten	___
5 die Bestellung erledigen/ausführen	___
6 den Auftrag ablehnen	___
7 die Bestellung zurückziehen	___
8 den Auftrag rückgängig machen	___

Exercises

1 Companies have ___ *(Auftragsbücher)* and established ordering routines.
2 They sometimes have to ___ *(sich bewerben)* for orders against their business rivals.
3 They may ___ *(gewinnen)* an order or ___ *(verlieren)* it.
4 As a rule, commercial orders ___ *(unterliegen)* certain conditions.
5 They have to be ___ *(abgesegnet)* and ___ *(überwacht)* before they are ___ *(aufgegeben)* and ___ *(bearbeitet)*.
6 Each order has to be ___ *(überprüft)* before it is shipped.

3.2 Tricky translations

Please translate:

1 Er tätigt seine Geschäfte überall auf der Welt.
2 Mit dieser Firma sollte man keine Geschäfte machen.
3 Sie zahlen ihre Schulden allmählich ab.
4 Wir lassen die überfälligen Außenstände durch ein Inkassobüro eintreiben.
5 Inzwischen hat die Firma eine Menge Schulden angesammelt.
6 Arbeiten Sie auf Kommissions- oder Provisionsbasis?
7 Sie sollten eine Schuldenberatung aufsuchen, um Ihre Schulden los zu werden.
8 Ist der Auftrag zu Ihrer Zufriedenheit ausgeführt worden?
9 Dieser Auftrag ging an ein internationales Konsortium.

3.3 Additional practice

1 Businesses and business deals: Collocations

- business/es: as a countable noun is synonymous with 'company/ companies', whose types are explained in III.2.1, note [14], p. 44.
- business: when used as a non-countable noun signifies 'business transactions'. The collocations *Geschäfte abschließen, Geschäfte machen* thus have to be translated as: to do business, to conduct business. In this context, it would be incorrect to use the plural. Alternative translations are: 'to clinch/make business deals'; 'to carry out business transactions'.

Examples of the singular noun vs. plural noun usage.

We have done a fair amount of business in this area.

He opened several businesses in the north of England.

The exercises below demonstrate that there are a large number of collocations for both the countable and the non-countable variant of 'business'.
Consult your dictionaries and/or pick the English equivalent from the box below.

acquire • close down • downsize • give up • go out of • manage • open • represent • reengineer • run • run down • sell • supply with • take over

	eine Firma gründen	to set up a business
	erwerben	____
1	erwerben	____
2	eröffnen	____
3	betreiben	____
4	leiten	____
5	beliefern ... mit	____
6	übernehmen	____
7	umstrukturieren	____
8	verschlanken	____
9	vertreten	____
10	veräußern	____
11	bankrott machen	____
12	aufgeben	____
13	zu Grunde gehen lassen	____
14	schließen	____

Compare the above collocations to those that can be formed with 'business deal' below. Look at the words in the box if necessary.

approve • cancel • delay • insure • negotiate • review • wreck • turn down

	ein Geschäft abschließen	make/clinch/close/pull off a deal
1	aushandeln	____
2	genehmigen	____
3	ablehnen	____
4	aufschieben	____
5	annullieren	____
6	ruinieren/in den Sand setzen	____
7	versichern	____
8	überdenken	____

2 Business: idioms

Please translate the following idioms into German.

1 Let's get down to business.
2 Mind your own business.
3 This is none of your business.
4 This is a tricky business.
5 They managed to drum up some extra business over Easter.
6 He sped down the road like nobody's business.
7 I'm afraid I have to attend to some other business first.
8 This is purely a business matter.
9 We are tired of the whole business.
10 I am afraid he means business.

XI Payment Methods in Foreign Trade

XI Payment methods in foreign trade

Das Dokumentenakkreditiv ist die am häufigsten verwendete Zahlungsweise im Außenhandel. Der Grund für seine Beliebtheit ist die Tatsache, dass dabei die eventuellen Risiken für alle beteiligten Handelspartner auf ein kalkulierbares Minimum reduziert werden.

Jedoch ist der Exporteur der eigentliche Begünstigte, da er am meisten von der von zwei anerkannten internationalen Banken verbrieften Zahlungssicherheit profitiert. Doch auch der Importeur hat die Gewissheit, dass die von ihm bestellten Waren seinen Anweisungen entsprechend versandt wurden.

Zunächst vereinbaren Exporteur und Importeur einen Kaufvertrag sowie die Modalitäten des Akkreditivs. Danach beauftragt der Importeur seine Bank, ein Akkreditiv auszustellen, das von der Bank des Begünstigten bestätigt wird. Die krediteröffnende Bank weist die Bank des Exporteurs an, dem Begünstigten den vereinbarten Betrag auszuzahlen, vorausgesetzt, dass dieser eine Reihe von genau beschriebenen Dokumenten vorlegt, die den Versand des Handelsgutes und die Verfügungsgewalt über die Lieferung anzeigen.

Sind die vorgelegten Dokumente vollständig und einheitlich ausgefüllt, erfolgt unverzüglich die Auszahlung an den Exporteur. Diese Vorgehensweise wird auch als „Zahlung bei Vorlage" bezeichnet. Anschließend informiert die Bank des Exporteurs – die sogenannte avisierende Bank – ihre Partnerbank über den aktuellen Stand. Die gebilligten Dokumente gehen nun an die Partnerbank und von dort an den Importeur, der damit die Auslieferung der Waren erwirkt.

Sind die Unterlagen fehlerhaft, wird dem Exporteur eine bestimmte Frist gesetzt, diese Mängel zu beheben. Kann er diese nicht einhalten, muss er die Auslieferung der Ware verzögern oder sie gegebenenfalls rückgängig machen.

Dokumentenakkreditive sind von großer Bedeutung für Exporte in krisengeschüttelte Gebiete und für Neulinge im internationalen Markt. Wegen den damit verbundenen Zahlungs- und Liefergarantien, und dem sich daraus ergebenden erhöhten Zeit- und Verwaltungsaufwand sind Akkreditive allerdings auch recht kostenintensiv und umständlich für alle Beteiligten.

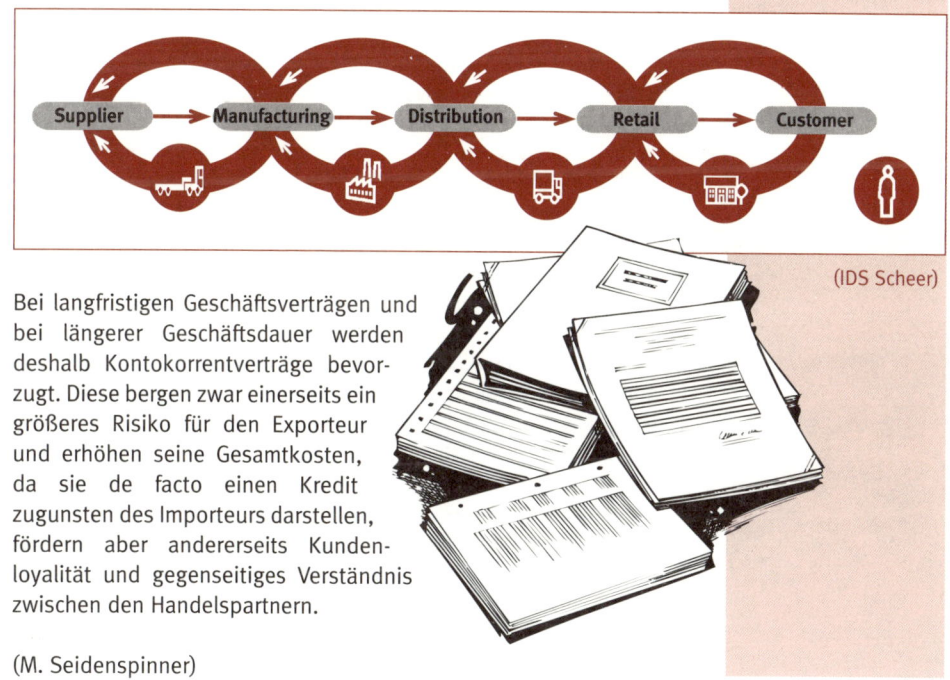

(IDS Scheer)

Bei langfristigen Geschäftsverträgen und bei längerer Geschäftsdauer werden deshalb Kontokorrentverträge bevorzugt. Diese bergen zwar einerseits ein größeres Risiko für den Exporteur und erhöhen seine Gesamtkosten, da sie de facto einen Kredit zugunsten des Importeurs darstellen, fördern aber andererseits Kundenloyalität und gegenseitiges Verständnis zwischen den Handelspartnern.

(M. Seidenspinner)

Documentary (letter of) credit[1] versus open account agreement[2]

The documentary letter of credit is the most commonly used method of payment in foreign trade. The reason for its popularity lies in the fact that **this method**[3] reduces the **potential**[4] risks for all **parties involved**[5] to **a quantifiable**[6] minimum. However, it is the exporter who is the **actual beneficiary**[7] as he profits most from the **payment guarantee**[8] **provided in a contract**[9] by two **reputable** international **banks**[10]. But the importer, too, can be certain[11] that the goods ordered have been **dispatched**[12] according to his instructions.

At the outset[13], exporter and importer agree on a **sales contract**[14] as well as on the **terms**[15] of the documentary credit. The importer then **commissions**[16] his bank **to issue**[17] a letter of credit, which is confirmed by the beneficiary's bank. The issuing bank instructs the exporter's bank to pay out the agreed amount to the beneficiary **provided that**[18] he presents a number of **precisely specified**[19] documents which state when the consignment was shipped and who exerts the **power of control**[20] over the **consignment**[21].

If the documentation submitted is complete and **consistent**[22], **payment is made**[23] without further delay. This procedure is referred to as 'payment on presentation'.

The exporter's bank – **also known as**[24] the advising bank – subsequently **notifies**[25] its partner institution about the current status. The approved documents are now passed on to the issuing bank and from there to the importer, **who uses them to effect delivery of his consignment**[26]. If the documentation is faulty, the exporter is given a **deadline**[27] **to rectify these deficiencies**[28]. If he cannot meet this deadline, he has to delay delivery of the consignment or – if need be – even **reverse**[29] the shipment.

Documentary credits are of great significance for exports to **crisis-stricken areas**[30] or for newcomers to the international marketplace. However, owing to the payment and shipment guarantees **which they include**[31] and the additional amount of time and **administrative work**[32] **which they entail**[33], L/Cs are, however, also somewhat cost-intensive and **cumbersome**[34] for all parties concerned.

This is why, in long-term business agreements and for longer periods of trading[35], preference is given to open account agreements. **Although, on the one hand, these involve**[36] a higher risk for the exporter and – as they **represent**[37] de facto trading loans in favour of the importer – increase his total cost, **on the other hand, they encourage**[38] customer loyalty and mutual understanding between the trading partners.

2.1 Notes on the translation ● ● ● ● ● ● ● ● ●

1 *Dokumentenakkreditiv:* documentary letter of credit; documentary credit; letter of credit; L/C

> The 'letter of credit' is issued by one bank and sent to another. It authorizes the payment of a sum stated in it to the person named in it.

← Please note

2 *Kontokorrentvertrag:* open account agreement

> 'Open account agreements' are the most common payment method in domestic trade. They are usually carried out as follows: Goods are ordered, shipped and delivered before payment is made within an agreed period of time. The 'credit period' may stretch from 30 to 120 days in certain countries or business areas. 'Open accounts' predominantly benefit the customer and can be vital in terms of customer retention. However, they add substantially to the cost incurred by the supplier.

← Please note

3 *dabei:* this method ...;
Students will find this sentence easier to translate if they rewrite it in the active voice.
For details on *dabei* see VI.3.3, Exercise 2, p. 88.

4 *eventuell:* potential

> The adverb 'eventually' is a false friend. It is nearly synonymous with 'in the end', 'finally', but not a translation of *eventuell* which means 'perhaps', 'maybe'. *Eventuell* can also be rendered by 'may' or 'might'.
> Example
> *Dieses Thema wird eventuell morgen zur Sprache kommen.*
> This topic might be discussed tomorrow.

5 *für alle Beteiligten:* for all parties involved; for all parties concerned
'Concern' used as a verb corresponds to *betreffen, zutreffen*.
Example
This does not concern our company. *Das betrifft unsere Firma nicht.*
Compare
This does not apply to our company. *Das trifft auf unsere Firma nicht zu. Das gilt nicht für unsere Firma.*

●●●●●●●● The phrase 'To whom it may concern' *(An alle, die es angeht)* is the heading of testimonials or open references destined e.g. for future employers.

For further semantic implications of 'concern' see V.2.1, note [10], p. 69 and VI.2.1, note [25], p. 84.

[6] *kalkulierbar, berechenbar:* quantifiable; calculable; predictable

[7] *eigentlicher Begünstigter:* actual beneficiary; real beneficiary
Alternatively: Strictly speaking, however, it is the exporter who is the beneficiary

[8] *Zahlungssicherheit:* payment guarantee; guaranteed payment; secured payment

Please note →

> *Sicherheit* denotes a variety of related semantic entities.
> - *Sicherheitsvorschriften:* 'safety regulations', usually those which aim at protecting the workforce, e.g. in hazardous shop floor areas
> - *Sicherheitskräfte:* 'security guards', who take precautions to protect a person or an organisation against crime
> - *Gewissheit:* 'certainty', which refers to the condition of being certain or of having proof (see note [11] below).

For *sichern* see I.2.1 note [25], p. 17.

[9] *der verbrieften:* provided in the contract; laid down in/stated in/ guaranteed in the contract

[10] *anerkannte Banken:* reputable banks; banks of repute; banks of good standing/of good reputation

[11] *doch auch der Importeur hat die Gewissheit:* but the importer, too, can be certain; but the importer, too, can be sure/has proof
For the translation of the impletive *doch* see XI.3.3 Additional practice, Exercise 1, p. 156.

[12] *versandt:* dispatched; shipped
- to dispatch: to send off from the point of departure where the transportation process begins
- to ship, to transport: i.e. to carry out the entire transportation process from departure to destination

For 'mail' and 'mailing' see II.2.1, note [27], p. 33.

[13] *zunächst:* at the outset; at the beginning; first

[14] *Kaufvertrag:* sales contract; sales agreement

[15] *Modalitäten:* terms; conditions

[16] *beauftragt:* commissions; instructs; advises
Cf. I.2.1, note [20], p. 16.

[17] *ausstellen:* to issue; to open

18 *vorausgesetzt, dass:* provided that; on condition that
19 *genau beschriebenen:* precisely specified; specifically described
20 *Verfügungsgewalt:* power of control
This authorises a person or organisation to handle the merchandise during the process of transportation.
21 *Lieferung:* consignment

> *Lieferung* can stand for various interrelated semantic units, namely, 'consignment', 'delivery', 'shipment'.
> * *(an-/zu-)gelieferte Ware:* the goods supplied
> * *Warenlieferung, Warensendung, zu versendende Ware:* consignment (of goods)
>   'Consignments' are 'packaged and dispatched goods'.
>   'Consignment' can also denote the 'act of shipping goods'.
>   Examples
>   We regret to inform you that your consigment was damaged due to a rail accident.
>   Has the cooler consignment arrived yet?
>   We have commissioned an agent for the consignment of goods to foreign countries.
> In commercial documents, an agent receiving shipped merchandise would be referred to as the 'consignee', whereas the principal supplier of the consignment would be called 'consignor'.
> * *Auslieferung:* delivery
>   'Delivery' refers to the fact that the consignment has changed hands and ownership. The point of destination and the time of delivery therefore play a major role in sales negotiations.
>   *ausliefern:* to effect delivery; to make delivery; to deliver the goods
> * shipment, transportation
>   'Shipment' signifies 'carriage' or 'transportation of goods' by a carrier, a haulage company or a freight forwarder.
>   In international usage, 'shipment' can also denote 'the goods shipped'.

← Please note

22 *einheitlich ausgefüllt:* consistent
The full translation of *einheitlich ausgefüllt,* namely, 'filled in (out) in a consistent fashion' seems cumbersome.
23 *erfolgt ... die Auszahlung:* payment is made; payment is executed/effected

●●●●●●● [24] *sogenannt:* also known as; aka; also referred to as

> The direct rendering 'so-called' could be misleading in this context as this expression tends to mean *vorgeblich, angeblich*.

[25] *mitteilen:* to advise; to notify
Hence: *die avisierende Bank:* the advising bank

[26] *der damit die Auslieferung der Waren erwirkt:* who uses them to effect delivery of his consignment
For *Auslieferung* see note [21] above; for possible translations of *dabei, damit, davon* see VI.3.3 Additional practice, Exercise 2, p. 88.

[27] *Frist:* deadline

> Note the following collocations
> *eine Frist setzen:* to set somebody a deadline, to give somebody a deadline
> *eine Frist einhalten:* to meet a deadline

[28] *diese Mängel beheben:* to rectify these deficiencies; to correct these errors/mistakes

Please note →

> - 'deficiency'
>   covers all types of 'imperfections', 'shortcomings' *(Unzulänglichkeiten)*, 'defects' and 'flaws'
> - 'mistake'/'error'
>   'To err is human', and 'mistakes' or 'errors' are generally made by people.
>   Examples
>   typing error, typing mistake: *Tippfehler*
>   spelling mistake, spelling error: *Orthographiefehler*
>   behavioural error: *Verhaltensfehler*
>   human error: *menschliches Versagen*
>   Related usage
>   learning by trial and error: *durch 'Ausprobieren' lernen*
>   error analysis: *Fehleranalyse*
>   Let's err on the right side. *Lassen Sie uns auf Nummer 'Sicher' gehen!*
> - 'faults': *Fehler, Mängel* (plural noun; see also: 'shortage' below)
>   'Faults' are deficiencies inherent in materials, equipment and processes. Human beings can have 'faults' too.

Usage examples

Konstruktionsfehler: design fault

Nobody is perfect. We all have our faults.

It's not our fault (i.e. 'we are not to blame').

- 'defect': a lack of completeness or perfection; inbuilt deficiency in materials, equipment and human beings.

Examples

production defect: *Produktionsfehler*

zero defect production: *Produktion mit einer Fehlerquote von Null*

These components are all defective. *Diese Teile sind alle defekt (d.h. schadhaft).*

character defect: *Charakterfehler*

- 'flaw': an inherent deficiency; a blemish; a crack

flawed material / a flaw in the material: *Materialfehler*

flawless material: *makelloses, fehlerfreies Material*

a flawed diamond: *kein lupenreiner Diamant*

a flawed process: *fehlerhafter Prozess*

flawed information: *inkorrekte Information*

- 'shortage', 'scarcity': a lack in the amount required: *Mangel* (no plural form)

- 'weakness': a weak link (in a chain), a weak point: *Schwäche; Schwachstelle*

Related adjectives

fehlerhaft: deficient; faulty; flawed; full of mistakes

schadhaft: defective; flawed; faulty

---

[29] *rückgängig machen:* reverse; recall

[30] *krisengeschüttelte Gebiete:* crisis-stricken areas; crisis-ridden regions

[31] *den damit verbundenen:* which they include; their inherent ...

For the translation of modifying adjectival phrases such as *den damit verbundenen*, see VI.3.3 Additional practice, Exercise 2, p. 88.

[32] *Verwaltungsaufwand:* administrative work; red tape

'Red tape' is a colloquial idiom for time-consuming, superfluous and bureaucratic work.

[33] *sich daraus ergebend:* which this entails; resulting from this

Cf. VI.3.3 Additional practice, Exercise 2, p. 88.

[34] *recht umständlich:* somewhat cumbersome; rather inconvenient

●●●●●●●● 35 *bei längerer Geschäftsdauer:* for longer periods of trading; for longer trading periods

36 *diese bergen zwar einerseits ...:* although, on the one hand, these involve

37 *darstellen:* represent; constitute

38 *fördern aber andererseits:* on the other hand, they encourage
Cf. VI.2.1., note 22, p. 84 for the translation of *fördern*.

XI.3 Exercises

3.1 Terminology: Delivering and paying

1 Please complete the sentences below by using the terms and expressions provided in the above text and notes.

1 With ___ *(Kontokorrentzahlungen)* the ___ *(Kreditperiode)* can stretch from 30 to 120 days. This ___ *(begünstigt)* above all the customer.

2 From the ___ *(Versandort)*, the goods are ___ *(versandt)* to the ___ *(Zielort)*.

3 ___ *(Auslieferung)* makes reference to the fact that the ___ *(Warenlieferung)* has been transferred to the hands of the new ___ *(Besitzer/in)*.

4 The L/C is the safest ___ *(Zahlungsweise)* for ___ *(alle Beteiligten)*.

5 A cheque, which is paid ___ *(nach Sicht)* to the ___ *(Überbringer)*, is a type of ___ *(Akkreditiv)*.

6 This payment method is increasingly being replaced by ___ *(Kreditkarten)*, which are ___ *(sonst auch)* referred to as ___ *(Plastikwährung)*.

7 The ___ *(Lieferung)* was not ___ *(versandt)* before yesterday.

2 Using a monolingual as well as a bilingual dictionary, look up the appropriate English terms for the following:

zahlbar bei Aufforderung	payable on request/on demand
1 zahlbar bei Fälligkeit	___
2 zahlbar bei Lieferung	___
3 zahlbar bei Vorlage	___
4 zahlbar an Überbringer	___
5 Zahlungsaufforderung	___
6 Zahlungsbedingungen	___
7 Zahlungsbilanz	___
8 Zahlungserinnerung	___
9 Zahlungsfähigkeit	___

10 Zahlungsweise ____
11 Lieferschein ____
12 Lieferbedingungen ____
13 Liefertermin ____
14 Lieferant ____
15 Lieferzeit ____
16 Liefergarantie ____
17 Lieferzusage ____
18 Empfangsbestätigung ____

(© PIB Copenhagen)

3.2 Tricky translations

1 'To err is human ...'
   Translate the following sentences. Use the words given in (brackets).

1 Der Kunde wurde angewiesen, die angegebenen Daten zu vereinheitlichen. (ensure the consistency of)
2 Zu schnell zu fahren war wirklich ein Fehler. (definitely)
3 Hier liegt ein Materialfehler vor. Es handelt sich um schadhaftes Material.
4 Die Sicherheitsbestimmungen sollen die Belegschaft schützen. (workforce)
5 John arbeitet als Wachman im hiesigen Supermarkt. (security guard)
6 Der Vertrag trat letztes Jahr in Kraft. Er bleibt zwei Jahre gültig und läuft dann aus. (come into force)

2 Contracts

Find the English equivalent of the following collocations.

> cancel • extend • initial • negotiate • honour • implement •
> renew • sign • terminate

	einen Vertrag aufsetzen	to draw up an agreement/a contract
1	aushandeln	____
2	abzeichnen	____
3	unterschreiben	____
4	einhalten	____
5	umsetzen	____
6	erneuern	____
7	verlängern	____
8	annullieren	____
9	beenden	____

3.3 Additional practice: doch

Words such as *'schon', 'doch', 'denn'* frequently do not constitute independent semantic entities or convey little meaning in a German sentence. Their meaning and their usage sometimes escapes foreign learners completely. The semantically highly complex *doch* is a typical case in point. Obviously, there is no <u>one</u> translation for this impletive.

- The emphatic *doch* can be rendered by a phonetic stress on a supportive auxiliary, followed by a question tag.
  Examples
  Die Lieferung kommt doch morgen? The consignment will arrive tomorrow, won't it?
  Es funktioniert doch? It does work, doesn't it?
- The contrasting *doch* replaces *nicht nur ... sondern auch* constructions.
  Examples
  Nicht nur Sie sondern auch wir freuen uns...
  Doch auch wir freuen uns ... But we, too, are looking forward to ...
- The contradicting *doch*:
  Examples
  Doch, das ist die beste Zahlungsweise.
  No, but this is the best method of payment.

- The didactic *doch* functions like an admonishing raised index finger.
  Das funktioniert doch nicht.
  Believe me/Look/Now look, this is not going to work.
- The reproachful *doch* suggests that one has knowingly/ deliberately overstepped a limit or broken a promise, although one should know better.
  Du sollst doch dort nicht parken.
  You know perfectly well I have told you not to park here.
  Du wolltest doch die Zahlen überprüfen.
  But you promised you'd check the figures.
- The conclusive *dann aber doch, schließlich doch* can be rendered by 'eventually', 'finally', 'in the end'.
  Der Kunde war nicht gerade erpicht auf ein Akkreditiv, aber schließlich stimmte er doch zu.
  The customer was not too keen on a letter of credit but he agreed in the end/... but he eventually/finally consented.

Now translate the following sentences. There is bound to be more than one option.
1 Eventuell ist es doch noch möglich, die Bestellung zu stornieren.
2 Und wenn wir den Auftrag nun doch verlieren?
3 Doch auch für den Kunden hat dieses Verfahren Vorteile.
4 Er ist nun doch nicht gekommen.
5 Das geht doch nicht.
6 Vielleicht akzeptieren sie unseren Vorschlag doch?
7 Du wolltest das doch für dich behalten.

XII Markets and Mergers

XII Markets and Mergers

Fusionen sind längst keine amerikanische Spezialität mehr. Auch in Europa ist die Konsolidierung in einzelnen Branchen weit fortgeschritten. Bei Pharma, Automobil, Banken, Rückversicherungen und Telekommunikation sind nach Unternehmensaufkäufen und Zusammenschlüssen die Märkte fest in der Hand relativ weniger Wettbewerber.

Eine Branche bleibt in Europa deutlich zurück: die Konsumgüterindustrie. Doch neuerdings verstärken sich die Signale, dass der atomisierten Branche eine Fusionswelle bevorsteht, wie sie etwa die europäische Pharmabranche gerade durchlebt hat. Marginales Marktwachstum und knappe Margen machen den Konsumgüterherstellern das Leben schwer. Vielfach verdienen nur noch die *Category Leaders* auskömmliche Renditen. Doch über organisches Wachstum ist die Marktführerschaft kaum zu erreichen – bleibt der Ausweg über Zukäufe und Zusammenschlüsse.

Der Grad an Konzentration der Konsumgüterbranchen in den wichtigsten europäischen Ländern ist gering. Mit knapp 15 Prozent Marktanteil der zehn bedeutendsten Unternehmen liegt er zum Beispiel bei Nahrungsmitteln und Getränken signifikant unter dem Niveau anderer Branchen, wie zum Beispiel Pharma mit jeweils 35 Prozent oder der Autoindustrie mit gar 91 Prozent.

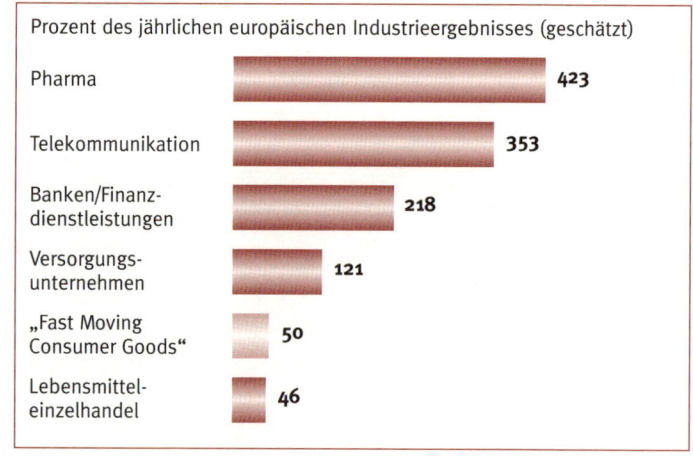

Prozent des jährlichen europäischen Industrieergebnisses (geschätzt)

Pharma	423
Telekommunikation	353
Banken/Finanzdienstleistungen	218
Versorgungsunternehmen	121
„Fast Moving Consumer Goods"	50
Lebensmitteleinzelhandel	46

(McKinsey & Company, Inc.)

160

Die geringe Konzentration vieler Produktsegmente in europäischen Märkten hat keine strukturellen Gründe. Genau diese Kategorien sind nämlich in den USA hoch konzentriert. So haben zum Beispiel die drei größten Brauereien in Europa gerade 24 Prozent Marktanteil, während die Top-Drei in den USA 73 Prozent des Marktes halten. Bei Brot betragen die Anteile der drei Größten acht Prozent in Europa und 28 Prozent in den USA, bei Fleischprodukten zwölf Prozent in Europa und 58 Prozent in den USA.

Zwang zum Wachstum: In den meisten Branchen der *„Fast Moving Consumer Goods" (FMCG)* haben sich die zweistelligen Wachstumsraten von Umsätzen und Renditen aus den achtziger Jahren in der Zwischenzeit mehr als halbiert. Zum einen liegt dies an der schwachen Entwicklung der Nachfrage. So ist etwa der Anteil der Ausgaben für Lebensmittel, Getränke und Genussmittel an den Gesamtausgaben der Verbraucher zwischen 1985 und 1996 in Deutschland um fünf Prozentpunkte (von 23 auf 18 Prozent), in Frankreich um drei (von 21 auf 18 Prozent) und in Großbritannien um fünf Prozentpunkte (von 25 auf 20 Prozent) gesunken. Zum anderen ist in vielen Unternehmen ein Großteil der möglichen Kostensenkungspotentiale durch die umfangreichen internen Restrukturierungsprogramme der letzten Jahre ausgeschöpft.

(quoted from Dellago, V., Thomas, C., Tochtermann A., and Voss, W.-D.: „Die nächste Fusionswelle trifft Europas Konsumgütermarkte", in: *McKinsey akzente 12 consumer & service industries*, McKinsey, Juli 1999)

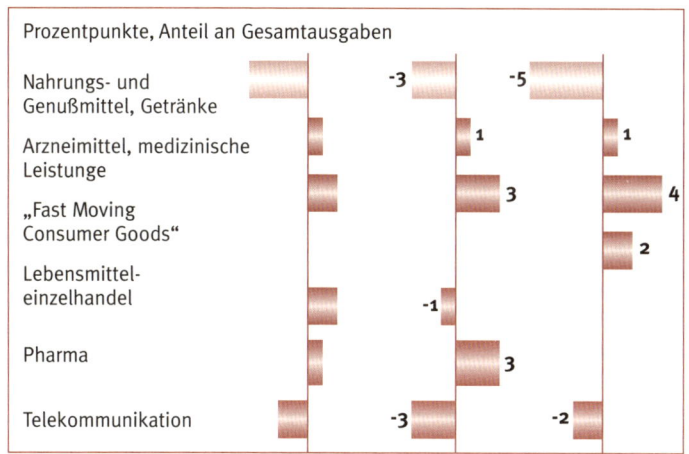

Prozentpunkte, Anteil an Gesamtausgaben

Nahrungs- und Genußmittel, Getränke   -3   -5

Arzneimittel, medizinische Leistunge   1   1

„Fast Moving Consumer Goods"   3   4

   2

Lebensmitteleinzelhandel   -1

Pharma   3

Telekommunikation   -3   -2

(McKinsey & Company, Inc.)

The next wave of mergers[1] will take place in[2] Europe's consumer goods[3] markets

Mergers[4] are no longer an American speciality. In Europe, too, consolidation within the individual **industrial sectors[5]** has made substantial progress. **In the wake of[6]** company mergers and **acquisitions[7] in pharmaceuticals[8], the automotive industry[9]**, banking, reinsurance and telecommunications, the markets are **firmly under the control[10]** of a relatively small number of competitors.

One sector remains significantly behind in Europe: the consumer goods industry. However, the indications have recently become stronger that **this highly fragmented sector[11] is about to see a wave of mergers[12]** similar to that which has just been experienced in the pharmaceuticals industry, for example. **Minimal[13]** market growth and **low margins[14]** are making life difficult for the manufacturers of consumer goods. In many cases, it is only the category leaders who **are** still **earning adequate returns[15]**. However, **market leadership is very unlikely to be achieved by organic growth[16]** – the only solution thus lies in acquisitions and mergers.

There is a low **degree of concentration[17]** in the consumer goods industries in the most important European countries. **In the food and beverages industry[18]**, for example, where the ten largest companies hold a market share of **just under 15 per cent[19]**, it is significantly lower than in other sectors, such as pharmaceuticals (where the ten largest companies hold 35 per cent) or the automotive industry (where they hold **as much as 91 per cent[20]**).

This low degree of concentration in many product segments in the European markets **does not have any structural causes[21]. For in the USA it is in precisely these product categories that market concentration is high[22].**

To take one example, the three largest breweries in Europe have a market share of just 24 per cent, whereas the top three in the USA hold a market share of 73 per cent. The three largest bread producers in Europe have an eight per cent market share, compared with 28 per cent in the USA; in the meat products sector, the top three manufacturers in Europe hold a market share of twelve per cent, compared with 58 per cent in the USA.

In most sectors of the fast-moving consumer goods (FMCG) industry, the double-figure growth rates in turnover and profits of the nineteen eighties **have been more than halved[23] since then[24]**. On the one hand, this is related to **the weak growth in demand[25]. Expenditure on[26] food, drink and tobacco[27]**, for example, **fell[28]** by five percentage points from

23 per cent to 18 per cent of total consumer expenditure in Germany between 1985 and 1996; in France it fell three percentage points (from 21 per cent to 18 per cent), and in Great Britain: five percentage points, from 25 per cent to 20 per cent. On the other hand, many companies have now exhausted most of their **potential for cost-cutting**[29], following the large-scale internal restructuring programmes of recent years.

2.1 Notes on the translation

●●●●●●●●●

1 *Fusionswelle:* wave of mergers; spate of mergers; series of mergers; merger wave
   See also note [4] below.

2 *trifft:* will take place in; will be in; will affect; will have an impact on

> The simple future form is used, as this is a forecast. The verb 'to hit' would be inappropriate, as it means 'to have a negative effect on', and this is not indicated by the text which follows.

3 *Konsumgüter:* consumer goods; consumption goods

← Please note

> 'Consumer goods' are goods in everyday use that are purchased by members of the public. They consist of:
> - 'consumer durables' *(Gebrauchsgüter, dauerhafte Güter)*, also called 'durables', 'durable goods', 'durable consumer goods', 'hard goods', which have a relatively long lifetime, such as cars, washing machines or computers,
> - 'consumer nondurables' *(Verbrauchsgüter, kurzlebige Konsumgüter)*, also called 'nondurables', 'nondurable consumer goods', 'disposables', which have a relatively short lifetime, such as food, perishable goods *(leicht verderbliche Waren)*, newspapers or clothing.
>
> Note that goods traded in 'business-to-business markets' are referred to as 'capital goods' *(Investitionsgüter)*.

4 *Fusion:* merger; amalgamation

← Please note

> Both 'merger' and 'amalgamation' translate *Fusion, Zusammenschluss, Verschmelzung.*
> - 'merger': In its precise sense, this term means the combination (merging) of two or more companies on an

equal footing and by mutual agreement in order to create a new business entity. In this case no party is the acquirer or the acquired.

- 'amalgamation', the more general term, may be a merger, an acquisition, or a newly created company which takes over the previously combined ones.

5 *Branche:* industrial sector; industry; sector of industry; business sector; sector; branch of industry; branch of business
See V.1.2, note [13], p. 70

6 *nach (Unternehmensaufkäufen und Zusammenschlüssen):* in the wake of; following a wave of; after a series of/a wave of; as a result of
'In the wake of' indicates that something occurs after and because of something else.

7 *Unternehmensaufkauf:* acquisition; takeover

Please note →

> Unlike 'mergers', 'takeovers' are usually mounted by one firm which makes a hostile takeover bid *(feindliches Übernahme-angebot)* without seeking the agreement of the acquired company's management.
> 'Acquisitions' can be: firstly, 'horizontal takeovers' *(horizontale Akquisitionen)* of direct competitors, secondly, 'vertical takeovers' *(vertikale Akquisitionen)* of customers' or suppliers' operations, and thirdly, 'conglomerate takeovers' *(konglome-rate Akquisitionen)* of business organisations operating in unrelated markets.

> One company is 'acquired' ('bought', 'purchased', 'taken over') by another company, which seeks to expand its market or to diversify its activities, for cash and/or equity.

8 *bei Pharma:* in pharmaceuticals; in the pharmaceuticals sector/industry

> Note the plural form. In some compounds, *Pharma* may also be translated as 'drug(s)'.
> Examples
> *Pharmaunternehmen:* pharmaceuticals company, drugs company
> *Pharmahersteller:* drugs manufacturer

⁹ *(bei) Automobil:* (in) the automotive industry; (in) the auto/ automobile industry; (in) the car industry
'Auto/automobile' tends to be used more in American English, 'car' more in British English. The adjective 'automotive', which relates to road vehicles, is used in both American and British English.

¹⁰ *fest in der Hand (von):* firmly under the control of; under the firm control of; firmly in the hands of
'Well in hand' has a different meaning: If something is 'well in hand', it is 'well under way', 'approaching completion'.
Example
The preparations for next month's conference are well in hand.

¹¹ *die atomisierte Branche:* this highly fragmented sector; this fragmented industry

> 'Fragmented' means consisting of several separate parts. 'Highly fragmented' conveys the idea implied in *atomisiert* that these parts are very small.
> 'To fragment' a market or industry means 'to split it up'/'break it up' into small segments/units.
> Note the use of the pro form 'this' (instead of 'the') to highlight the connection to the word 'sector' (or 'industry') in the previous sentence.

¹² *dass der ... Branche eine Fusionswelle bevorsteht:* that this ... sector is about to see a wave of mergers; that this ... sector is about to be faced with a wave of mergers; that in this ... sector there is about to be a wave of mergers; that in this sector there will soon be a wave of mergers

¹³ *marginal(es Wachstum):* minimal; a very low rate of; marginal
'Minimal' and 'marginal' both mean very slight, very small. 'Minimal' is preferred here simply to avoid a clumsy juxtaposition of 'marginal' and 'margins'.

¹⁴ *knappe Margen:* low margins; narrow margins; tight margins; low/ narrow/tight profit margins
The opposite of all these terms is 'high margins'.

¹⁵ *auskömmliche Renditen verdienen:* are earning adequate returns; are making adequate profits

> Note that the progressive form is employed in this and the previous sentence because this is a description of a current situation, not of a general rule or principle.

●●●●●●●●

'Yield' is also a translation of *Rendite* but would not be appropriate here. As a financial term, it denotes the 'income from an investment', e.g. in a stock or equity.

16 *über organisches Wachstum ist die Marktführerschaft kaum zu erreichen:* market leadership is very unlikely to be achieved by organic growth; it is hardly likely that market leadership will be achieved by/through organic growth; a company is hardly likely to/very unlikely to achieve market leadership through organic growth

Please note →

'Market leaders' hold the largest market share and are usually associated with 'market dominance' *(Marktbeherrschung)*. As a rule, their pricing policies, distribution coverage and promotional spending impact directly on those of the 'market followers' *(Marktfolger)* who wish to maintain their market share with considerably lower investment costs. A 'market challenger' *(Marktherausforderer)* is a company that has the second largest market share and aggressively strives for market leadership.

17 *Grad an Konzentration:* degree of concentration; concentration ratio; measure of concentration

Please note →

The 'degree of concentration' is the percentage of the market supplied by a given number of the producers in a specific industry. We can say, for example, that the European car industry is highly concentrated, or more precisely, that the ten-firm concentration ratio is 91 per cent. This may be used as an indicator of the degree of competition in a market. An alternative approach to assessing competition is to look at the market share of each of the largest firms.

18 *bei Nahrungsmitteln und Getränken:* in the food and beverages industry; in the F & B industry/business; in the food and drink industry

Please note →

- 'Food' is used both as a special-purpose term for *Nahrungs-mittel* or *Lebensmittel* and as a more general term for *Essen, Nahrung, Kost, Futter.*
- 'Beverages' is the formal counterpart of 'drinks' and thus more likely to be used in this context.
  Commercial collocations with food are
  food processing: *Lebensmittelverarbeitung*

> food labelling: *Lebensmittelkennzeichnung*
> food retailing: *Lebensmitteleinzelhandel*
> food wholesaling: *Lebensmittelgroßhandel*

● ● ● ● ● ● ● ●

[19] *knapp 15 Prozent:* just under 15 per cent; slightly less than 15 per cent; a little less than 15 per cent
(Note that the pattern of the original text has to be considerably changed in order to produce a clear and understandable English sentence.)

[20] *gar 91 Prozent:* as much as 91 per cent
Alternatively: '... it is significantly lower than in other sectors, such as pharmaceuticals or the automotive industry, where the market shares of the ten largest companies amount to 35 and 91 per cent respectively.'
For specific practice with quantifiers such as *gar* see 3.3, Exercise 1, p. 172.

[21] *hat keine strukturellen Gründe:* does not have any structural causes; is not caused by structural factors

[22] *genau diese Kategorien sind nämlich in den USA hoch konzentriert:* for in the USA, it is in precisely these product categories that market concentration is high; for it is precisely these categories/segments that are highly concentrated in the USA

> Note that, in both alternatives, a 'cleft sentence', namely: 'It is precisely ... that ...' is helpful for the translation of *genau dies/e*.

[23] *haben sich mehr als halbiert:* have been more than halved; have been cut by more than 50 per cent; have been cut by more than half
See also VIII.3.3 Additional practice: reflexive verbs, p. 116.

[24] *in der Zwischenzeit:* since then
For the correct grammatical usage of 'since then' see VII.2.1 note [20], p. 98.

[25] *die schwache Entwicklung der Nachfrage:* the weak growth in demand; the poor growth in demand; the weak increase in demand; the falling off of demand; the slowing/slackening/weakening of demand; the slackness in demand; the slack demand

[26] *der Anteil der Ausgaben für:* expenditure on

> In dictionaries, learners will find the following translation suggestions for *Ausgaben*: expenditure, total expenditure, cost (of), outlay

← Please note

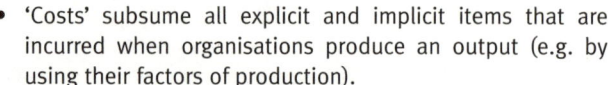

- 'Costs' subsume all explicit and implicit items that are incurred when organisations produce an output (e.g. by using their factors of production).
- 'Outlay' is synonymous with costs although it is a more formal and also a specific financial term, e.g. used in investment analysis, where it has the distinct meaning of 'money invested'.

Example

This project will require an initial outlay/investment of £100 000.

The semantic aspects of 'expenditure' include:

the 'act of spending'

the 'amount spent or expended'

the 'total amount spent by a company within a business period'.

For reasons previously explained (see VII.2.1, note [3], p. 95), the dogmatic distinction between Ausgaben and Aufwendungen is of less relevance in Anglo-American businesses. The German terms can best be translated as follows:

- *Ausgaben:* total expenditure, total spending, total spend.
  'Total expenditure' subsumes all 'outflowing amounts' *(Geldausgänge)* which reduce a company's 'financial assets' *(Geldvermögen)* by using its time and resources. It includes all costs and expenses incurred when achieving a company's 'gross income'.

> Note that 'spending' is uncountable and that 'expenditure' is mostly used in its singular form. In US usage, the synonymous neologism 'total spend' (noun) is steadily gaining ground.

- *Aufwand, Aufwendungen:* expense, expenses; cost of; also: expenditure This item represents the periodical amounts expended on material, equipment and services which a company has to purchase in order to achieve 'revenues' (Erträge; see VII.2.1, note [3], p. 95).
  'Expenses' comprise – among other items – the 'cost of sales' *(Kosten der zur Erzielung der Umsatzerlöse erbrachten Leistungen)*, which are, first and foremost, the cost of 'raw and ancillary materials' *(Materialaufwand und Aufwendungen für Hilfsstoffe)* and of 'consumables' *(Betriebsstoffe)*, the 'salaries and wages' *(Gehälter und*

Löhne), the 'contributions to social security and pensions' as well as 'other operating expenses' *(sonstige betriebliche Aufwendungen)*. Moreover, they include the cost of 'components' purchased for resale *(Fremdbauteile)* and of 'external services' *(Fremdleistungen)*, 'the selling expenses' *(Vertriebskosten)*, 'cash' or 'volume discounts' *(Skonti oder Boni)* and 'damage losses' *(Verluste aus Schadensfällen)*.

Examples

Any expenses that you incur in order to attend the interview will be covered. *Alle Aufwendungen, die Ihnen entstehen, um am Interview teilzunehmen, werden erstattet.*

Travel expenses are charged to our expense account. *Reisespesen werden dem Spesenkonto belastet.*

Our expenditure on software was very high last year. *Unser Aufwand für Software war im letzten Jahr sehr hoch.*

[27] *Lebensmittel, Getränke und Genussmittel:* food, drink and tobacco; food, beverages and tobacco

> *Genussmittel*, used by itself, may be translated as 'luxury foods and drinks and tobacco' (which is not very elegant), but there is no single English term which corresponds exactly to it.

[28] *(der Anteil der Ausgaben) ist gesunken:* expenditure fell; expenditure dropped/decreased

← Please note

- When referring to figures, levels (e.g. of inflation), standards, temperature, the translation of *'sinken'* is usually 'fall', 'drop' or 'decrease'.
- When referring to currencies, profits, numbers of people, sink seems to imply a slight note of regret.

Examples

The euro sank even further against the dollar on Friday.

The population of … is sinking.

Profits have sunk since last year.

For further practice on the interpretation of figures see X.2.1 note [7], p. 137.

[29] *mögliche Kostensenkungspotentiale:* potential for cost-cutting; cost-cutting/cost-reducing potential, potential for cost-reduction; possibilities for cost-cutting/cost-reduction

Please note that 'potential' has no plural form and that 'possible potential' would be a tautology in English.

3.1 Terminology: mergers, markets and consumption

1 Complete the sentences below, using appropriate terms from the sample translation and the notes.

1 The widely publicized Mannesman-Vodaphone ___ *(Fusion)* was in fact a ___ ___ *(feindliche Übernahme)* of an industrial giant by a dynamic, shrewd and powerful ___ / ___ *(Konkurrent/Rivale)*.

2 Academic studies of the big ___ *(Fusionierungswellen)* of this century have shown that the shareholders of ___ ___ *(übernommener Gesellschaften)* have benefited, while those in the ___ ___ *(übernehmenden Gesellschaften)* have lost.

3 Trying to make the ___ *(fusionierten)* companies work often proves to be a great managerial challenge.

4 Clearly, a significant benefit is that the two partners can ___ *(erweitern)* their ___ ___ *(Marktanteil)* and perhaps ___ *(erreichen)* ___ ___ *(die Markführerschaft)*.

5 The marriage of the two ___ *(Pharmahersteller)* was called off before it reached the altar.

6 ___ *(die Nachfrage)* has ___ *(nachgelassen)*, which has led to decreasing ___ *(Umsätze)* and ___ *(Renditen)*.

7 This product ___ *(verkauft sich)* like hot cakes; we have never had one that was more marketable.

2 Find translations of the terms below which are related to 'market', 'sales' and 'consumption'. Make use of the footnotes and of dictionaries where necessary.

	Marktbeherrschung	market dominance
1	Marktanalyse	___
2	Marktchance	___
3	Marktprognose	___
4	Marktposition	___
5	Marktsegmentierung	___
6	Marktfähigkeit	___
7	konsumierbar	___
8	Verbrauch, Konsum	___
9	Verbraucher, Konsument	___
10	Endverbraucher	___
11	Gebrauchsgüter	___
12	Konsumgüter	___

3.2 Tricky translations

1 Costs

Please translate:

1 Kennen Sie eigentlich den Unterschied zwischen 'kostenwirksam' (d.h. sich auf die Kosten auswirkend), 'kostenintensiv' (d.h. hohe Kosten verursachend), 'kostengünstig' (das heisst zu einem niedrigen Preis), 'kostensenkend' (d.h. die Kosten reduzierend), und 'kosteneinsparend' (d.h. weniger Kosten erzeugen)?

2 Diese Entscheidung scheint uns ausschließlich kostenmotiviert zu sein. Die Mitarbeiter haben dabei keine Rolle gespielt.

3 Die Berechnung aller Kosten für ein Fertigprodukt wird im Englischen als „Costing", die Berechnung des Verkaufspreises dagegen als „Pricing" bezeichnet.

4 Das Wort ‚Unkosten' kommt zwar in einigen deutschen Redewendungen vor, ist aber kein betriebswirtschaftlicher Fachbegriff.

Die wertvollsten Marken der Welt	
1992	**1996**
1 Marlboro	1 Coca-Cola
2 Coca-Cola	2 Marlboro
3 Intel	3 IBM
4 Kellogg's	4 McDonald's
5 Nescafe´	5 Disney
6 Budweiser	6 Sony
7 Pepsi	7 Kodak
8 Gillette	8 Intel
9 Pampers	9 Gillette
10 Bacardi	10 Budweiser
11 Winston	11 Nike
12 Levi's	12 Kellogg's
13 Newport	13 AT&T
14 Motorola	14 Nescafe´
15 Kodak	15 General Electric
16 Camel	16 Hewlett-Packard
17 Nike	17 Pepsi
18 Campell's	18 Microsoft
19 L'Orèal	19 Frito-Lay
20 Hennessy	20 Levi's

☐ FMCG
☐ nicht FMCG

(McKinsey)

2 Translating German present tenses

Translate the following sentences into English. Pay attention to the key words which function as indicators for the correct tense.

Examples

Knappe Margen machen uns zur Zeit das Leben schwer. Low margins are making life difficult for us.

Fusionen sind längst alltäglich in Europa. Mergers have long since become common in Europe.

Neuerdings verstärken sich die Signale. The signals have recently become stronger.

1 Eine Branche bleibt immer zurück.

2 Unser Umsatz steigt neuerdings wieder: Wir profitieren von dem Konjunkturaufschwung.

3 Marshal Motors baut (derzeit) für rund 15 Millionen Dollar ein neues Werk in Brasilien.

4 Die Vorbereitungen für die Produktionsaufnahme laufen jetzt an.

5 China bleibt für uns weiterhin das bedeutendste Absatzgebiet.

6 In letzer Zeit verkaufen sich unsere Backwaren sehr gut.

7 Wir bilden schon längst weibliche Führungskräfte aus.

8 Unser Unternehmen ist seit langem auf den südostasiatischen Märkten etabliert.

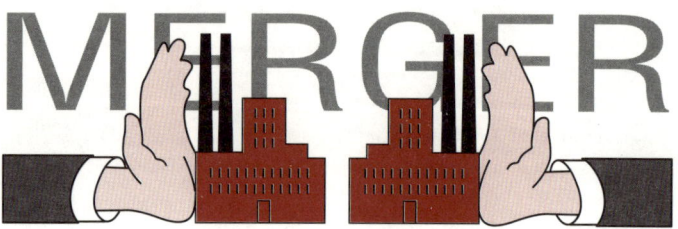

3.3 Additional practice

1 *sogar/gar*

The quantifying adverb *sogar* is often translated by 'even' but this is by no means the only possibility.

• *Sogar* firstly is a <u>qualifiying attribute</u> that accompanies nouns, pronouns and adjectives (mostly for emphasis) – in which case it is synonymous with *selbst/auch* and can be translated as 'even'. In negative sentences, it is synonymous with *nicht einmal* ('not even').

• Secondly, *sogar/gar* is a <u>quantifying apposition</u> which accompanies measurable and countable quantities. In such cases, it has no synonym and translates as 'as high as', 'as many as', 'as much as', etc.

• In many cases, the quantifying *sogar* can simply be treated as an impletive or "semantic space filler" which requires no translation.

Now make an informed choice with the following examples.

1 ___ cash-rich companies are in need of innovation.

2 The succeeding product was ___ more expensive.

3 In Great Britain, costs fell by ___ five percentage points

4 In the automotive industry the degree of concentration is ___ 91 per cent.

5 He was extremely helpful and ___ lent us his car.

6 The ten largest companies have a market share of ___ 95 per cent.

7 Not ___ state-owned enterprises are exempt from taxation.

8 ___ 3% discount would be too little.

2 Adverbial modifiers

In German, noun attributes are often modified by adverbials such as *möglichst, gänzlich*. On translating these qualified attributes it may be advisable to convert them into relative clauses or gerund forms.

Example

eine high-tech gesteuerte Anlage: a plant (which is) controlled by high-tech equipment/machinery

ein gänzliche unbekannter Hersteller: a producer who is completely unknown

Note that if modifiers are adverbials of time (e.g. *längst, zur Zeit*) they may be indicative of a certain tense.

Translate the following sentences.

1. möglichst parallele Produktionsprozesse
2. die damit verbundenen höheren Kosten
3. die unseretwegen verschobene Sitzung
4. die daraus entstandenen Nachteile
5. das zur Zeit entstehende Kraftwerk
6. ein vollkommen revidiertes Verfahren
7. anders denkende Kollegen
8. die verloren geglaubte Lieferung
9. die von der Firmenleitung bekannt gemachte Mitteilung
10. der ursprünglich umgesetzte Plan
11. die heute getroffene Vereinbarung
12. eine längst vergessene Begebenheit
13. die noch zu zahlenden Gehälter
14. die sehr spät eingetroffene Nachricht
15. sein vor zehn Jahren gestorbener Geschäftspartner

Appendix

Key

I Telephone Banking

1
1 standing order/banker's order
2 bank statement/account statement
3 carried out
4 current account/checking account
5 (account) balance
6 safeguard/cover
7 secure/protect
8 share/stock dealing(s)

2
1 savings account/deposit account
2 joint account
3 numbered account
4 account number
5 account holder
6 credit card
7 bank/financial institution
8 borrower
9 credit facilities/credit facility/credit line
10 overdraft
11 blank cheque
12 open cheque/uncrossed cheque
13 crossed cheque
14 to make out a cheque/to write out a cheque
15 to cash a cheque
16 a (credit) transfer order
17 transferee/credit transfer remittee
18 credit transfer form/credit transfer slip
19 (credit) transfer charge
20 credit transfer payments/cashless transfer payments/bank transfers
21 securities/stocks and shares
22 investment in securities/investment in stocks and shares
23 securities portfolio
24 portfolio management
25 investment advice/investment consulting

definition	translation
1 a loan for which an asset (such as a house) is used as a guarantee in case the loan is not repaid	*ein gesichertes Darlehen*
2 a firm/solid starting position, from which further progress can be made	*eine sichere Ausgangs-position*
3 an investment which is not risky; a sound investment	*eine sichere (Kapital-)Anlage/ eine sichere Investition*
4 to keep for future use, or to avoid wasting	*sparen, einsparen*
5 rescue	*bewahren/retten*
6 make secure, close firmly, fasten	*sichern/fest (ab)schließen*
7 money saved	*Ersparnisse*
8 people who save money, e.g in a bank account	*Sparer(innen)*
9 present/latest	*aktuell*
10 real/true	*tatsächlich*
11 (reduced) prices offered on goods or services	*(Sonder-)Angebote*
12 amount/range available to buy or use	*Angebot*
13 act of asking for something, esp. politely/formally	*Anforderung/Bitte*
14 statements about what to do	*Anweisungen/Anordnungen*

2   1   We will be pleased to handle/take care of/deal with your financial transactions.

    2   Our local branch will deal with your orders to buy or sell securities.

    3   Were our staff informed about the guidelines for online transactions/ business?

    4   Please store/save the new adresses.

    5   With your cash card/bank card you can use our cash dispensers/cash machines/cashpoints/automated teller machines at any time.

    6   Has my last credit transfer already been recorded on my statement?

    7   Your account was completely inactive/dormant last year. Don't you want to close it?

    8   How can I protect my savings more effectively/better?

    9   Please carry out our instructions exactly.

1

1 During business hours you can speak/talk personally to one of our staff.
2 You are welcome to arrange a personal discussion/meeting with our branch manager.
3 The telephone computer understands you best if/when you speak clearly and not too slowly.
4 You should change your PIN number/pincode immediately.
5 You need the right/correct account number.
6 You have not filled in/filled out the form correctly/properly/in the right way.
7 Cybercash provides a safe, fast and extremely convenient system of payment.
8 You can easily obtain the necessary software from the Internet free of charge.

2

1 from seven am/7 am/seven in the morning till three pm/3 pm/three in the afternoon
2 five days a week
3 open 24 hours (a day)
4 closed on Wednesdays
5 from six till eleven every evening/from 6 pm till 11 pm every evening
6 open (at) weekends
7 from dawn till dusk/from sunrise till sunset
8 from 10 am till 10 pm every day/from ten in the morning till ten in the evening every day
9 never on Sundays

II The Postal Service

1

1 whole/wide/broad range; delivery; registered letters and parcels/registered mail
2 service industry/service sector
3 medium/means/form
4 maintain; contacts
5 confidential; sent; envelope
6 sending/mailing/posting; trade samples; cost-effective
7 parcel; proof of posting
8 delivery times

2
1. postal delivery/mail delivery
2. postmark
3. stamped addressed envelope/s.a.e.
4. prepaid envelope/business reply envelope
5. postage paid/post-paid
6. international money order
7. business reply
8. business reply card
9. reply coupon
10. correspondence
11. letterhead
12. body/text of the letter
13. memo(randum)/note
14. postal address; mailing address
15. forwarding address
16. (of a letter or parcel:) recipient/addressee; (of goods:) consignee/recipient/receiver
17. sender
18. parcel/package
19. parcel post
20. parcel delivery
21. express parcel

1

Tricky translations
Words easily confused

	definition	translation
1	get in touch	sich melden/in Verbindung setzen
2	put ... through (on the phone).	jmd. verbinden/durchstellen (am Telefon)
3	touch; communication	Kontakt/Verbindung
4	contacts; people (who can help)	Beziehungen/Verbindungen
5	regular; long-term; not temporary	festangestellte (Mitarbeiter)
6	regular; frequent	ständig/regelmäßig
7	all the time, very often	ständig/(an)dauernd
8	without interruption	ständig/durchgehend/ununterbrochen
9	severe-looking; with a serious expression on his face	ernst dreinschauend/dreinblickend
10	properly/correctly designed and executed, with a businesslike appearance, not amateurish	professionell aussehend/seriös aussehend

11 bad, big, considerable, not slight	*ernst/ernstzunehmend/schlimm*
12 a suggestion to be taken seriously	*ein ernstzunehmender/ernstge-meinter Vorschlag*

2 1 These constant/continual interruptions make it difficult to concentrate.

2 Is 10 Downing Street your permanent address?

3 We worked continuously from 8 am till 8 pm to get this task finished.

4 The sales figures have improved steadily/continuously since last year.

5 Is this information reliable?

6 Jack certainly won't let you down – he's extremely reliable/dependable.

7 Promex is a reputable/professional firm and a serious contender for the contract.

Additional practice **1** 1 Our branches are being modernised all the time./Our branches are constantly / continually being modernised.

2 Our business is becoming increasingly internationalised./Our business is becoming more and more internationalised.

3 This technology is constantly/continually being improved.

4 The market for services is growing/expanding faster and faster.

5 His performance at work is getting better and better:/His performance at work is improving all the time.

6 The costs are continually/constantly increasing./The costs are increasing all the time./The costs are getting higher and higher.

2 1 The evidence/proof is not conclusive/definite/clear.

2 Is all this mail/post for me?

3 The goods have not been delivered up till now/so far yet.

4 We have ordered fifty (items/units)./We have ordered fifty of them.

5 The electronic media are gradually replacing the traditional letter.

6 E-mail is an electronic means/medium/form of communication which is used by many people.

7 Our headquarters were moved/transferred to London.

8 Is this data / information confidential?

9 The information was not very helpful.

III Teleworking

Terminology **1** 1 employees/workers/staff

Workforce and work 2 workplace/company/office

environment 3 desk/workstation/telework space

4 premises
5 different
6 difference
7 at the company/in the company's offices/at work
8 plant/factory
9 undertaking/business/enterprise/venture
10 company/firm

2 1 job environment/working environment
2 working life
3 work permit
4 data processing
5 data protection
6 database, data bank (data bank = a collection of databases)
7 data capture, data acquisition, data collection
8 customer behaviour (US behavior)
9 after-sales service, customer service, back-up service
10 customers, clientele
11 customer service
12 customer loyalty
13 regular customer, (regular) patron (of a restaurant/hotel)
14 company doctor (US company physician)
15 tour of the plant, plant visit
16 plant closure for the holidays, (US vacation close-down)
17 works outing, company outing
18 works/factory/plant manager
19 office equipment
20 office supplies
21 office space, office premises, office accommodation
22 office building, office block
23 office hours

1

Tricky translations
Words easily confused

	definition	translation
1	market in the producer's own country	*Inlandsmarkt*
2	volume of goods sold in the seller's own country	*Inlandsabsatz*
3	machines used in the home	*Haushaltsgeräte*
4	computer used in the home/family	*Heimcomputer*
5	business activity/venture	*Unternehmen*

6	industry, business activities	*(Privat)Wirtschaft, Industrie*
7	private ownership of companies	*freies Unternehmertum*
8	to create employment	*Arbeitsplätze schaffen*
9	to create an area for working	*(sich) einen Arbeitsplatz einrichten/schaffen*
10	at (the place of) work	*im Betrieb, am Arbeitsplatz*
11	(independent) advice/information for potential buyers/end-users	*Verbraucher-/ Konsumentenberatung*
12	advice/help/information for clients of a company	*Kundenberatung*
13	a supplier of costumes	*Kostümverleih, Kostümschneider*
14	of approximately/of about/of around	*von etwa/circa/ungefähr*
15	near/in the area of/not far from	*in der Nähe von*
16	area to live (or work):	*Nachbarschaft/Gegend/Viertel*
17	the closeness	*die unmittelbare Nähe, die kurze Entfernung*

2 1 This seminar will familiarise you with essential negotiation techniques.

2 Communication technology nowadays has to be user-friendly.

3 The customer has given us an important commission which has to be carried out within the next three weeks./The customer has placed an important order with us which has to be executed in the next three weeks.

4 The company's premises are in close proximity to the shopping precinct.

5 The (purchasing) price is in the vicinity of £5 million.

Additional practice   **1** 1 There are four main forms of teleworking.

2 Internet travel agencies have existed for quite a long time.

3 Last year, there were some problems with the deliveries.

4 It was a question of whether the government would use the revenue to reduce the budget deficit.

5 Several problems still have to be solved./There are still several problems to be solved.

6 There were several important tax reforms between 1994 and 2000.

7 Ten letters had to be answered./There were ten letters to be answered.

8 There will be many different forms of work in the future.

9 It is about ten kilometres to the airport.

2　1　I have been dissatisfied with his performance for some time.

2　We have been in the black/We have been making a profit since July.

3　Many jobs have been lost since the merger.

4　What have you been doing recently/lately?

5　I have been in London a lot recently/lately.

6　Since applying/since she applied for the job, she has not heard any more/anything further.

7　Since the firm was taken over, profits have been falling./Since being taken over, the firm's profits have been falling.

IV Intercultural Communication

1　1　agree more

2　agreed to

3　agree about

4　agreed on

5　agreed with

6　Is it agreed that

7　as agreed

Terminology
Agreements

2

1	*anstreben*	seek
2	*treffen*	conclude
3	*einhalten*	abide by (gesetzliche Verpflichtung)
		honour (ethische Verpflichtung)
4	*verletzen*	infringe
5	*brechen*	break
6	*umgehen*	bypass
7	*widerrrufen*	revoke

1　1　He was obviously unable to come.

2　This is a tough nut for us to crack.

3　This was hitting below the belt.

4　We ought to meet halfway.

5　The company felt obliged to honour the agreement.

6　The customers made no complaints whatsoever.

7　Our competitors did not betray the smallest sign of weakness.

8　Are you prepared to make concessions/to compromise?

9　I am beginning to have second thoughts about this decision.

10　He remained adamant in his decision.

Tricky translations

2
1. He is said to be/considered to be punctual and efficient.
2. Our rival is reputed/said to be a fair opponent, and so he is.
3. This task is supposed to be very simple.
4. The company is supposed/reputed/said to supply high quality merchandise.
5. He is thought/said/reputed to be a good colleague.
6. He reckons he is a good organiser.
7. The luggage is believed to have been forwarded to Paris.
8. Managers are generally assumed to/thought to/believed to think rationally.
9. He is said/supposed to have agreed.

Additional practice
Pinpointing the problem

1. in a nutshell
2. item
3. full stop/period
4. bulletpoints
5. on the dot/sharp
6. Point (taken!)
7. detail
8. four point six
9. dotted line
10. no point in
11. dot
12. soft spot
13. point of no return

V Management

Terminology

1
1. competitors/rivals; referred to; emulation
2. economies of scale; decrease/reduction; unit costs
3. achieved; factors of production; labour costs; competitive advantages; location
4. SME; acquired a reputation; conglomerate
5. credited; entrepreneurs
6. competitiveness

2
1. results; met; sales targets; exceeded
2. objectives; broaden/expand
3. goal; implement
4. development aid; aims; maintain; exhausting
5. success; failure

184

1   Economies of scale are expected to result in reduced unit costs.   Tricky translations
2   Core competencies are of strategic importance for every corporation.
3   This procedure is 'best practice' in the wood processing industry.
4   Successful managers have to have hands-on experience, perform excellently and practise what they preach.
5   The company needs a change of paradigm.
6   The German 'Mittelstand' is credited with being highly competitive all over the world.
7   How can Germany regain its attractivenes as a business location?
8   The right corporate culture is said to boost staff motivation and to facilitate identification with the company.
9   The systems approach is related to chaos theory.

1   How long have you known this?   Additional practice
2   The meeting does not start until ten to three.   *schon, nur, erst*
3   This is the third time he has phoned today.
4   Industry did not start to benefit from the advantages of automisation until the beginning of the 20th century.
5   This has been our corporate motto for years.
6   Our head of department will manage somehow.
7   The film is being shown only today.
8   This question cannot be addressed until later.

VI Leadership Culture

1   issue; vision statement; values; perceives   Terminology
2   assess/evaluate   Values and evaluation
3   Human Resource Management; staff; performance appraisal
4   Value-led/value-driven; essential; quantitative objectives; human factor; corporate culture
5   executives; compartmentalisation
6   access; flow of knowledge/knowledge transfer; synergy effects
7   staff development
8   coined; practice; what he preaches

1   I went to the travel agency with a view to booking a flight to Japan.   Tricky translations
2   The Head of Personnel/HR Manager was intent on introducing a performance-related pay system.
3   The CEO was committed to exposing all senior managers to the (hands-on) experience of the shopfloor.
4   Have you seriously considered improving this process?

5   A destination/goal is not worth reaching unless you enjoy travelling/getting there.
6   The prospect of being confronted with criticism prevents many people from speaking their minds.
7   Staff development schemes aim at retaining experienced and committed/ motivated employees in the company
8   The company has succeeded in establishing a performance index as a permanent feature of Human Resources Management.
9   When it comes to forming long-term alliances with customers, language skills/linguistic competence are often a decisive factor.

Additional practice   1   1   A further conference was (supposed/meant) to be called in the following week.
2   We were (requested/asked/told) to present the new training scheme in today's meeting.
3   We were (expected/told/asked/requested/supposed) to submit the report today.
4   Was he actually (meant/supposed) to be informed?
5   This product was not (meant/destined) to survive in the market.
6   He was (destined) to die young.
7   This was (planned/intended/supposed/meant) to be a surprise for our new colleague.
8   The staff were (expected/invited/recommended/supposed to) to make suggestions for improvements.

1   Maybe you should/ought to have a look in your in-tray/mailbox.
2   We should/ought to do more for our employees.
3   He should/ought to put in an appearance at the meeting.
4   Surely our planning should/ought to be a little more efficient.
5   I feel that we should/ought to make enquiries.
6   You had better inform the customer.
7   You had better call in on/go and see the HR Manager immediately.

1   Do you want/Would you like me to arrange this/deal with/handle this for you?
2   Why did you want me to interview him?
3   Do you want/Would you like me to repeat this for you?
4   Do you want me to leave a message?/Would you like me to take a message?
5   Where would you like us to wait?
6   Would you like me to note down your telephone number?

2 1 while doing this/while opening the machine/in the process
  2 while paying attention to/while considering
  3 resulting from this, arising from this/which this entailed
  4 thereby/as a result/consequently
  5 at the same time/he also took this opportunity to mention
  6 this payment method

VII Human Resources Management

1 extensive; downsizing; reengineering/restructuring; cost-saving; job losses   Terminology
2 employee empowerment; responsibility; frontline   Managing change
3 delayering; affects
4 accountable
5 job satisfaction; job enrichment; job enlargement; productivity
6 severance pay; golden handshake
7 low-trust climate; involvement/commitment
8 high trust climate
9 put ... in the shade/dwarf

1 It is not my place/it is not up to me to judge your behaviour.   Tricky translations
2 The bus has 20 seats and a standing capacity of 35.   Places and spaces
3 Richard Branson reputedly clinches most of his business deals on the tennis court.
4 On Sundays, you will find Carl on his local football pitch.
5 We have a splendid view of 'Castle Square'.
6 Do take a seat.
7 We must make room/space for the new consignment.
8 Business process reengineering has made some companies more competitive but has also cost a lot of jobs.
9 Please put/leave your car in the new car park.
10 I am afraid Mr. Brown is not in his office.
11 John and Laura are currently sharing the same office space.
12 Make way!/Get out of my way!

1 significant/insignificant events   Additional practice
2 likely/unlikely story   Opposites
3 legible* – illegible text (i.e. difficult to decipher)
4 reproachable – irreproachable/impeccable manners
5 soluble – insoluble problem
6 deficient – impeccable/flawless/perfect quality

7 comprehensible – incomprehensible; understandable – impossible to understand
8 appropriate – inappropriate example
9 responsible – irresponsible decision
10 comparable results – results that cannot be compared
11 avoidable – unavoidable result
12 understandable – an answer which is not understandable
13 pardonable – unpardonable
14 dispensible/waivable – indispensible/unwaivable
15 imaginable – inconceivable/unimaginable
16 revocable – irrevocable letter of credit
17 accessible/inaccessible data
18 non-comparable – unequalled, unrivalled, unparallelled performance, incomparable *(ohnegleichen; einmalig)*
19 unlikely – incredible, unbelievable story
20 illegible –– unreadable text (which may well be legible but cannot be understood)
21 unrecognisable – unmistakable pictures

VIII Employee Participation

Terminology

Pay, performance and benefits

1 1 piece rate
2 compensation/pay/remuneration; link/tie
3 are paid; performance-related; bonuses
4 variable payments/variable pay: salaries
5 performance/profits/success; perks

2 1 perks/fringe benefits
2 contribution
3 subsidies/handouts/grants
4 allowance
5 bonus/gratuity
6 legacy/bequest
7 endowments/donations

Tricky translations

1 1 obtain; receive
2 obtained
3 obtaining
4 obtained
5 obtained/received

6   obtain

7   received

1   Each employee was allocated/given ten company shares.
2   We were sent your application by e-mail.
3   Last year, we were all awarded a pay increase.
4   Have you been given your holiday pay yet?
5   For this improvement, she was awarded a prize by the company.
6   The workers are paid their bonus in the month following the annual general meeting.
7   Each partner is allocated a share of the profits in proportion to his salary/a share in the profits which is related to the amount of his salary.
8   We have not yet been given a performance bonus.
9   He was granted an extra day's leave.
10 We have been allocated too little money for the advertising budget.

2 1   realised/made/achieved
2   are fetching/fetch
3   attained/obtained/achieved/have attained/have obtained/have achieved
4   reached
5   to have met with/to have achieved/to have had
6   yielded/has yielded/is yielding
7   achieve/attain/reach

1   *sich freuen auf*
2   *sich handeln um*
3   *sich benehmen*
4   *sich fertig machen/sich vorbereiten*
5   *sich langweilen*

Additional practice
Reflexive verbs

1   The customer is complaining/has complained about the late delivery.
2   Should you have any difficulty in operating the machine/device, please contact our service personnel/our after-sales service/our back-up service/ our service department.
3   Are you interested in the successor to this/that model?
4   We would be very pleased if .../to ...
5   I fear she was quite upset/annoyed by your remarks. I am afraid your comments made her quite angry.
6   Can we meet towards the end of the month?
7   I have to be sure/certain that I can rely on this date.
8   The price depends on the weight./The price is determined by the weight.
9   The sales figures have doubled; the expenses have been halved.

IX Process Management

1 1   failed; produce

2   congested; toll roads

3   eradicated; close-enough

4   aligning; superordinate

5   detection; prevention

6   assets; clarity; applicability; attainability

7   transparencies

8   interactive; multi-layered; lead times

9   design faults

2 1   occur/happen; surface; arise

2   be anticipated; be overlooked

3   ignore; go away/disappear; to tackle/attack

4   jumped/taken; overcome; pushed aside

5   solved; remain unsolved

6   knotty; a piece of cake

1   This sounds like a tall order. *Das hört sich nach einer schwierigen Aufgabe an. Das klingt schwierig.*

2   You are facing an uphill struggle. *Das wird mühselig. Da haben Sie noch einiges vor sich.*

3   We got ourselves in a tight spot. *Wir saßen (ganz schön) in der Klemme.*

4   We have no leeway when it comes to prices. *Wir haben keinen (Verhandlungs)spielraum bei Preisen.*

5   *Da liegt der Hase begraben!* This is where the problem lies.

6   *Vorbeugen ist besser als Heilen.* Prevention is better than cure.

7   *Sie reagierten erst, als das Kind in den Brunnen gefallen war.* They locked the stable door after the horse had bolted.

8   *Wir sind vom Regen in die Traufe gekommen.* This was a case of "out of the frying pan into the fire".

1   Process management presupposes that all business processes are carefully planned and designed.

2   Technologically speaking, these processes are expected to mirror/represent/reflect the state of the art.

3   Process planning is expected to be a useful all-purpose tool/instrument.

4   Clearly structured processes are easier to implement.

5   Sister companies and external partners are involved/are integrated in this process.

6 This type of process mapping ought to be shelved or scrapped.
7 Process management has to make sure that quality deficiences are avoided.
8 The process should be able to benefit from the wide range of expertise and experience available in the company.
9 It is the waste of time, materials, energy and efforts which makes production costs soar; ... which pushes up/drives up production costs.

1 by contrast
2 compared to
3 unlike
4 unlike/in contrast to
5 taking into account, taking into consideration
6 owing to/due to/as a result of/because of
7 thanks to/due to/owing to
8 in the wake of/as a result of
9 in view of/with regard to
10 as to/with regard to/as far as ... is concerned
11 in this respect
12 in the course of
13 by way of introduction
14 according to
15 according to

Additional practice
More adverbials

X Enquiry Agencies and Debt Collectors

1 1 the deal was made/clinched/concluded; to make enquiries; solvency
2 agent; commission
3 dealer
4 distributor/concessionaire; end users; retailers
5 set up a business; wholesaling
6 terms of payment and delivery; buyer; seller; merchandise; payment
7 payer; payee

Terminology
Trading and ordering

2 1 to acknowledge receipt of
2 to confirm
3 to file; to store
4 to pass on
5 to carry out/to execute
6 to decline/refuse (to accept)/turn down
7 to withdraw
8 to cancel

1 order books
2 compete
3 win/obtain/be awarded; lose
4 are subject to
5 authorised; monitored, placed; processed
6 checked

Tricky translations

1 He conducts his business transactions all over the world.
2 You should have no business dealings with this company.
3 They are gradually paying off/paying back their debts.
4 We have commissioned a commercial collecting agency to recover our overdue outstanding accounts.
5 In the meantime, the company has accumulated a lot of/a large amount of debts.
6 Do you work on a sale-or-return or a commisssion basis?
7 You should consult a debt counsellor in order to get rid of your debts.
8 Has the order been executed/carried out to your satisfaction?
9 An international consortium was awarded this order.

Additional practice

1

acquire	open	run	manage	supply ... with
take over	reengineer	downsize	represent	sell
go out of	give up	run down	close down	
negotiate	approve	turn down	delay	cancel
	wreck/ruin	insure	review	

2
1 *Kommen wir jetzt zum Geschäftlichen.*
2 *Kümmere dich um deine Angelegenheiten.*
3 *Das geht dich nichts an.*
4 *Das ist eine komplizierte Angelegenheit.*
5 *Über Ostern konnten sie zusätzliche Kunden auftreiben.*
6 *Er rannte in Windeseile die Straße hinunter.*
7 *Leider muss ich mich zuerst um etwas anderes kümmern.*
8 *Das ist rein geschäftlich.*
9 *Wir haben die ganze Sache satt.*
10 *Ich fürchte, er meint es ernst.*

XI Payment Methods in Foreign Trade

Terminology
Delivering and paying

1
1 open account payments; credit period; benefits
2 place of departure; shipped; destination
3 delivery; consignment; owner

4 payment method; all parties concerned
5 at sight; bearer; documentary credit
6 credit cards; otherwise; 'plastic money'
7 consignment; dispatched

2
1	*zahlbar bei Fälligkeit*	payable at maturity
2	*zahlbar bei Lieferung*	payable on delivery
3	*zahlbar bei Vorlage*	payable on presentation
4	*zahlbar an Überbringer*	payable to bearer
5	*Zahlungsaufforderung*	demand for payment
6	*Zahlungsbedingungen*	terms of payment
7	*Zahlungsbilanz*	balance of payments
8	*Zahlungserinnerung*	prompt note (US), reminder
9	*Zahlungsfähigkeit*	solvency
10	*Zahlungsweise*	payment method
11	*Lieferschein*	delivery note
12	*Lieferbedingungen*	terms of delivery
13	*Liefertermin*	delivery date
14	*Lieferant*	supplier
15	*Lieferzeit*	delivery time/period
16	*Liefergarantie*	shipment guarantee
17	*Lieferzusage*	delivery promise
18	*Empfangsbestätigung*	delivery receipt

Tricky translations

1
1 The customer was advised to ensure the consistency of the data given.
2 Driving too fast was definitely a mistake.
3 This material is flawed. There is a flaw in the material.
4 Safety regulations are intended to protect the workforce.
5 John works as a security guard at the local supermarket.
6 The contract came into/entered into force last year. It will remain valid for two years, then it will expire.

2 negotiate • initial • sign • honour • implement • renew • extend • cancel • terminate

Additional practice
doch

1 But perhaps we can still cancel the order. But it might still be possible to cancel the order.
2 What if we do lose the order after all?
3 But this procedure is advantageous for the customer, too.
4 He has not come after all.

5 You know perfectly well that this is not going to work.

6 Maybe they will accept our proposal after all?

7 But you promised not to tell anybody!

XII Markets and Mergers

Terminology

Mergers markets and consumption

1
1 merger; hostile takeover; opponent/rival
2 merger waves; acquired firms; acquiring firm
3 merged, combined amalgamated
4 increase; extend; enlarge; market share; achieve; market leadership
5 drugs/pharmaceuticals manufacturers
6 demand; slackened/fallen off/slowed; turnover/sales; returns/profits
7 is selling

2
1 market analysis/survey
2 market opportunity
3 market forecast
4 market position
5 market segmentation
6 marketability
7 consumable
8 consumption
9 consumer
10 end user/end consumer
11 consumer durables/durables
12 consumer goods

Tricky translations

1
1 Are you actually aware of/do you actually know the difference between 'cost-related' (i.e. impacting on the costs), 'cost-intensive' (i.e. occasioning high costs), 'cost-effective' (i.e. provided at a low price), 'cost-cutting' (i.e. reducing the costs) and 'cost-saving' (i.e. resulting in/involving/entailing fewer costs)?

2 This decision seems to be exclusively cost-driven. The employer had nothing to do with it/played no part in it.

3 Calculating the costs for a finished product is referred to in English as 'costing', the calculation of the sales price, by comparison, is known as 'pricing'.

4 The word *'Unkosten'* occurs in quite a few German expressions; however, it is not a 'proper' business term.

2
1. One sector always remains behind.
2. Our turnover has increased/Our sales have increased again recently: we are benefiting from the cyclical upturn.
3. Marshal Motors is building a new factory in Brazil costing around 15 million dollars.
4. Preparations have begun/are under way/are beginning for the start of production/for the production start-up.
5. China continues to be/China remains/China is still our most important market.
6. Our bakery goods have been selling/have sold very well recently.
7. We have been training female/women managers for a long time now.
8. Our company has long since been established in the South-East Asian markets.

1
1. even
2. even
3. as much as
4. as high as
5. even
6. as much as/no quantifier
7. even
8. even

Additional practice

2
1. production processes which are as parallel as possible
2. the additional costs which this entails/has entailed
3. the meeting which was/has been cancelled because of us
4. the disadvantages arising from this
5. the power station (which is) currently being built
6. a procedure which has been completely revised
7. colleagues who are of a different opinion
8. the consignment which was assumed to be lost/to have been lost
9. the statement issued by the management
10. the plan (which had been) originally implemented
11. the agreement concluded today
12. an event which has long since been forgotten
13. the salaries that still have to be paid
14. the message, which has arrived very late
15. his business partner, who died ten years ago

acronym: a pronouncable name formed from a series of initial letters, e.g. "ASEAN" (Association of Southeast Asian Nations), "NATO" (North Atlantic Treaty Organization) or "NASA" (National Aeronautics and Space Administration)

adverb; adverbial phrase: a word or group of words that serves to modify a whole sentence by specifying the context of the verb e.g. in terms of time, place, intensity, condition and many other attributive features

analogy: an imitation of an existing liguistic pattern or model

ancillary construction: a supplementary and/or auxiliary structure *(Hilfskonstruktion)* such as *"dabei"* which acts as a grammatical supplement or substitute for full prepositional objects

apposition: a grammatical construction in which a noun phrase or noun is pre- or postposed to modify the meaning of another semantic item

attribute: an adjective or adjectival phrase that qualifies a noun, which in English can be preposed or postposed. Postposed qualifiers frequently create translation problems, e.g. "the details agreed on".

auxiliary verb: a verb used to indicate the tense (past, future), voice (active or passive) and mood (indicative, imperative, subjunctive) of another verb or to emphasise a statement made

clefting: breaks up information that could be given in a single clause into two clauses, which both have their own verb. "It is you, the MDs, who are supposed to set a good example".

collective noun: a singular noun that refers to a group of items or persons, e.g. "fruit", "furniture" or "humanity"

collocation: a combination of two unconnected lexical items which – as a result – form a semantically independent unit such as "an old hand" or "to meet targets"

compound: a word that consists of elements that are independent semantic, e.g. "leadership skills"

conjugated forms: the inflection of a verb – apparent in the verb ending – which indicate the person (first, second, third), the number (singular or plural), the tense (e.g. the present), the voive (active or passive) and the mood (imperative, subjunctive, indicative)

conjunction: group of words other than relative pronouns that connect sentences and other syntactical units, e.g. "and", "in spite of", "if", "whether"

connotation: an implied or suggested meaning; an association, a word that has an implied meaning; e.g. the word "unrest" denotes "social turbulence" but connotes "street riots"

declined forms: the inflected endings of nouns, pronouns or adjectives which state the case (e.g. genitive) and the number (singular and plural) of these items

denote: indicate, designate, to be a sign or symbol of something

derivative: a term which is based on another term in the same class. Zero-derivations, for instance, are verbs that derive directly from nouns (e.g. "carpet" – "to carpet")

emphatic: expressed (pronounced, spoken, read) or done with emphasis; having a distinct, distinguishing or sharp outline

euphemism: an inoffensive word or phrase substituted for one that is thought to be offensive, ill-mannered or hurtful, such as "to pass away" for "to die"

false friend: an incorrect linguistic analogy. This expression was coined by the French linguists Maxime Koessler and Jules Derocquigny in their 1928 publication *"Les faux amis ou les trahisons du vocabulaire anglais"*.

generic term: a term which is applicable to an entire class of nouns

homophones: words pronounced in the same way but differing in meaning or spelling

homonymies: two or several words that are spelt and/or pronounced in the same way but have different meanings

homonymic clash: misunderstanding or misconception due to homonymy

idiom: a group of words or a phrase whose meaning cannot be derived, or not entirely be derived, from its individual constituents (e.g. a "tall tale") which denotes a story that is hard to believe.

impletive: a semantic filler such as "actually" *(eigentlich)* or *"denn"* (in questions) that carries little or no meaning; impletives are mostly used for emphasis

intransitive verbs: verbs that are syntactically connected to the subject of a sentence which governs them. Some intransitive verbs cannot be followed by a direct object at all (e.g. "this problem surfaced all of a sudden"), others can switch from the intransitive ("he was walking up and down the room") to the transitive mode ("he was walking the dog").

inverted word order: a structure which changes the usual subject-verb-object order in a full sentence, e.g. whith certain qualifiers such as "little" ("little did he know", "hardly" ("hardly had he entered") or "not only" ("not only did he expect us to ... but he ...")

lexeme: a minimal semantic unit, such as "touch down" *(Landung)*, the meaning of which cannot be understood from its component morphemes "touch" and "down"

lexical item: a word listed in a lexicon or dictionary, a canonized or well documented linguistic item

metaphor: a figure of speech in which a semantic unit is applied to an object (person, item, action, abstract) that it does not denote; thereby a similarity is implied without being mentioned verbatim, e.g. "a tough cookie". Metaphors are related to similes or direct comparisons, e.g. "the jewel in the crown"; i.e. "the most cherished possession".

metonym: a figure of speech in which an attribute is used to hint at a more complex and comprehensive concept or issue, e.g. "he likes the bottle" instead of "he drinks too much"

modifier: a semantic unit that qualifies the meaning of a word or phrase; e.g. "this is highly unlikely", synonym: qualifier

morpheme: a speech element or semantic unit having a grammatical function that cannot be subdivided any further

neologism: a newly created word or term, a newly coined expression. Neologisms can be borrowed from other languages, such as *"der Cashflow"* in German and "mittelstand" or "waldsterben" in English or they can surface in one's mother tongue, e.g. "lean staff" *(verschlankte Mitarbeiter)*.

phonemes: sounds that constitute words; individual articulations that contribute to the significance of a word and which make it distinguishable from other word, e.g. "d" in "led" or the "t" in "let"

polysemous: a semantic unit that has several distinctly different meanings, e.g. "order"

postpositive modifier: a modifier placed after the word it qualifies

prepositional object: an object that is preceded by one or two prepositions, e.g. (let's talk) "to him", "about him"; (let's get "down to business")

prepositive modifier: a modifier placed before the word it qualifies

pro form: a personal or demonstrative pronoun or adverb substituting for another mostly longer noun or adverbial expression, e.g. "this" for "this matter" or "above" for "above-mentioned"

qualifier: see modifier

quantifier: a word that indicates a certain level, degree of intensity, or quantity of something; e.g. "much", "many", "a lot of"; "as early as"

reflexive verbs: verbs which refer back to the subject of a sentence or clause by means of a reflexive pronoun which is postpositive in conjugated verbs: "He could see himself in the dark window pane." *Er sah sich selbst in der dunklen Fensterscheibe.*

semantic: relating to the meaning of a word; arising from the distinctions between different words

subject: grammatical entity (noun or pronoun) that governs all other parts of an independent sentence and thus decides on its semantic contents.

subordinate clause: a lesser-order clause whose meaning depends on the superordinate sentence which it supplements: "They arrived but left shortly after. We would reconsider your proposal if we had time."

synechdoche: a figure of speech in which a part is substituted for the whole: "an old hand at engineering" for a person who enjoys considerable experience in engineering

synonym: a word or an expression that has a similar or identical meaning as another one, e.g. "hide" and "conceal". Synonyms often cover distinguishing nuances of the same semantic item but hardly ever mean exactly the same. They contribute substantially to the intricacies and idiosyncracies of natural languages.

syntax: the grammatical arrangement of words in a sentence or clause

term: a word used in a special purpose context or a specialized field of knowledge: *Begriff*

transitive verbs: the largest group of verbs. They need to be governed by an object to specify their meaning: e.g. "to stand a chance".

uncountable noun: a noun, such as "information" or "data", that has no plural form and cannot be preceded by an indefinite article

wh-words: words that introduce clauses, e.g. as interrogatives ("who, when, what, where, why", etc.) or as relativizers ("who, whom, which, where, why")

Reference Works & Further Reading

A Dictionary of Business, 2nd edition, Oxford University Press, Oxford, 1996

Adams, Scott, *Dilbert Gives You the Business,* Macmillan, London, 1999

Adams, Scott, *Das Dilbert Prinzip,* Heyne Verlag, München,1999

American Business Dictionary, Collin, P.H., et al., ed., Peter Collin Publishing, 1990

Bennis, W.,: *Managing People is Like Herding Cats: Warren Bennis on Leadership*, Kogan Page, London, 1998

Biber, Douglas, et al., *Longman Grammar of Spoken and Written English*, Pearson Education Ltd., Harlow, 1999

Cohen, J.M. and M.J.: *The New Penguin Dictionary of Quotations*, Harmondsworth, repr. 1998

Collins English Dictionary, 3rd edition, HarperCollins, Glasgow, 1991

Gallagher, John D., *Deutsch-englische Übersetzungsübungen*, 4. Auflage, München, 1996

Gibson, Robert, *Intercultural Business Communication: studium kompakt Fachsprache Englisch*, Cornelsen & Oxford, 2000

Gill, John, and Johnson, Phil, *Research Methods for Managers*, Paul Chapman, London, 1997

Glass, Neil: *Management Master Class: A Practical Guide to the New Realities of Business*, Nicholas Brealey, London, 1996

Goede, Gerd W., *Wirtschaftsenglisch-Lexikon*, Bd. 1-3, Oldenbourg Wissenschaftsverlag, München, 2000

Hamblock, Dieter, and Wessels, Dieter: *Großwörterbuch Wirtschaftsenglisch*, Cornelsen Giradet, Berlin, 1999

Handy, C., *Gods of Management: The Changing Work of Organisations;* Random House, London, 1991

Johnson, G., and Scholes, K.: *Exploring Corporate Strategy*, 4th edition, Prentice Hall, Hemel Hempstead, 1997

Kanter, R. M.: *When Giants Learn to Dance: Mastering the Challenges of Strategy, Management and Careers in the 1990s*, International Thompson Business Press, London, repr. 1996

Konstroffer, O., and Holke, C., *American job titles – und was sie bedeuten*, K&P International, Frankfurt am Main, 1996

Longman Dictionary of Contemporary English, 3. Ausgabe, Langenscheidt-Longman, München, 1995

LTP Dictionary of Selected Collocations, Hove, 1997

Hornby, A.S.: *Oxford Advanced Learner's Dictionary*, 5th edition, ed. J. Crowther Cornelsen & Oxford, Berlin, 1995

Pass, C. / Lowes, B. / Davies, L.: *Collins Dictionary of Economics*, 2nd edition.; HarperCollins, Glasgow, 1993

Percival, G. T., Donaghy, P. J., and Laidler, J. *European Charts of Accounts with English Translations*, Flambord Ltd. Europe, Durham, 1994

Peters, T. J., and Waterman Jr., R. H., *In Search of Excellence*, HarperCollins, Glasgow,1982, repr. 1991

Peters, T. J., and Waterman Jr., R. H., *Auf der Suche nach Spitzenleistungen*, Verlag Moderne Industrie, Landsberg, 1986

Rechnungslegung und Grundsätze der Abschlußprüfung in Großbritannien und Deutschland. Ein Vergleich/Accounting and Auditing Standards and Principles in the United Kingdom and

Germany: A Comparison, Price-Waterhouse GmbH, ed., IDW Verlag, Düsseldorf, 1995

Schäfer, Wilhelm: *Wirtschaftswörterbuch*, Bd.1-2, 6. Auflage, hrsg. von Michael Schäfer, Verlag Franz Vahlen, München, 1998

The American Heritage College Dictionary, 3rd edition, Boston, 1993

Veth, Klemens, and Lister, Ron, *Schlüsselbegriffe der Wirtschaft: studium kompakt Fachsprache Englisch*, Cornelsen & Oxford, Berlin, 1999

Index/Englisch

Index/Deutsch